VARIETIES OF AESTHETIC EXPERIENCE

Edited by
Earle J. Coleman
Virginia Commonwealth University

UNIVERSITY
PRESS OF
AMERICA

LANHAM • NEW YORK • LONDON

Copyright © 1983 by

University Press of America,™ Inc.

4720 Boston Way
Lanham, MD 20706

3 Henrietta Street
London WC2E 8LU England

Library of Congress Cataloging in Publication Data
Main entry under title:

Varieties of aesthetic experience.

Bibliography: p.
1. Aesthetics–Addresses, essays, lectures. I.
Coleman, Earle Jerome.
BH39.V32   1983   111'.85   83–6781
ISBN 0–8191–3276–4
ISBN 0–8191–3277–2 (pbk.)

*11 1.85
V312c*

TO MY CHILDREN

THOMAS and SARAH

iii

iv

ACKNOWLEDGMENTS

Grateful acknowledgment is made to thank the following person and publishers who have kindly granted me permission to quote from copyrighted works.

Monroe C. Beardsley, from Aesthetics: Problems in the Philosophy of Criticism (1958). Reprinted by permission of the author.

Clive Bell, from Art (1958). Reprinted by permission of G. P. Putnam's Sons.

Edward Bullough, "'Psychical Distance' as a Factor in Art and an Aesthetic Principle," from The British Journal of Psychology, Vol. 5 (1912). Reprinted by permission of the British Psychological Society.

Marshall Cohen, "Aesthetic Essence," from Philosophy in America, edited by Max Black (1962). Reprinted by permission of Cornell University Press.

John Dewey, from Art as Experience (1958). Copyright 1934 by John Dewey. Reprinted by permission of G. P. Putnam's Sons.

Jean-Paul Sartre, from Psychology of the Imagination, translated by Bernard Frechtman (1948). Reprinted by permission of the Philosophical Library Publishers.

D. T. Suzuki, from Zen and Japanese Culture (1959). Reprinted by permission of Princeton University Press.

CONTENTS

vii

viii

PREFACE

One recent introductory philosophy textbook, which states that it includes material representative of the major branches of philosophy, altogether omits reference to aesthetics. This omission is symptomatic of the fact that aesthetics has tended to be neglected or "shortchanged" by a majority of philosophers. Although many outstanding philosophers have made significant contributions to the study of aesthetics, it is simply true that, for the most part, philosophers have not devoted their greatest energies to the subject. Since theorizing about art and related phenomena has often been ignored, made subservient to other topics, or treated as something of a postscript in one's philosophizing, it is perhaps not surprising that the term aesthetics was not coined until the eighteenth century.

There are two conspicuous reasons why aesthetics has not enjoyed a place in the philosophical spotlight alongside the more established divisions of philosophy: metaphysics (theory of reality), epistemology (theory of knowledge), and ethics (theory of morality). First, the issues raised by the traditional philosophical disciplines strike one as being of

ix

more immediate concern or practical import: What is the
nature of reality? What is the nature of truth? and What is
the nature of the good life? An inquiry into the nature of
art, by contrast, impresses one as being of less urgency or
more of a luxury. Second, undoubtedly, numerous philosophers
have refrained from writing on aesthetics, because they lacked
a rich familiarity with the diverse art forms. Immanuel Kant
is a paradoxical exception to this last point in that his
minimal acquaintance with art did not prevent him from adding
considerably to the literature of aesthetics. What has been
termed the "contemporary explosion of the arts" is germane to
both points. The proliferation of new and widely-experienced
art forms such as the film, the pervasiveness of art today
(the tendency to place art works outside museums as in the
case of environmental sculpture or the museum without walls
phenomenon), and the growth of an ecological concern which
has shaped the art of architecture have all made art less
peripheral or tangential in our lives.

The purpose of the present book is to introduce the
reader to aesthetics, a topic which grows in relevance as
twentieth-century man finds himself bombarded by an ever-

increasing multiplicity of artistic expressions. The INTRODUCTION is divided into two parts. First a brief characterization of aesthetics is developed. While some anthologies avoid any attempt at definition, holding that any compact definition would be either whimsical or worthless, and other anthologies list crucial questions as a way of suggesting what aesthetics involves, this anthology will spell out the basic activities in which aestheticians engage. It is hoped that an account of such fundamental activities will provide a helpful introduction to the field.

The second part of the INTRODUCTION poses the question which is to remain thematic: What is aesthetic experience? My own views are presented in order to furnish a context for the readings which follow. Obviously, no single reply is apt to be definitive or exhaustive, but consulting a sampling of replies can expand one's understanding of aesthetic experience. Selections have been chosen on the basis of their ability to reflect the varieties of aesthetic experience. For example, a Japanese reading has been included in order to give a non-Western perspective. Each selection is preceded by intro-ductory comments.

I wish to express my gratitude to those who have made this work possible. Dr. Malcolm F. Stewarts' sensitivity and skill in introducing me to philosophy are greatly appreciated. I also wish to thank Professors C. Y. Chang, Monroe C. Beardsley (who was kind enough to read portions of my manuscript, make suggestions, and offer encouragement), George Dickie, John Hospers, and Jerome Stolnitz whose writings first acquainted me with aesthetics. Finally, I am deeply indebted to my wife for her interest and support.

INTRODUCTION

What is aesthetics? "Aesthetics is double-talk." Those who criticize aesthetics as being marked by fuzzy or vague thinking would be prone to support such an answer. But even aestheticians themselves would subscribe to this statement, given that it were properly qualified. Qualification is necessary, since to say "Aesthetics is double-talk" is to engage in double-talk, for "double-talk" means that which is ambiguous or nonsensical. No aesthetician would agree that all propositions in the literature of aesthetics are either obscure or meaningless. Thus, the aesthetician can speak of aesthetics as double-talk only in some third as yet unspecified sense. This sense will be clarified as the roles of the artist, appreciator, critic, and aesthetician are discussed.

Before moving to a positive characterization of what philosophers mean by the term "aesthetics," it may be valuable to discover what aesthetics is not. Putting the matter differently, it may be best to approach the issue through a process of elimination. What should be ruled out as descriptive of aesthetics in the philosophical sense? Consider the

following three activities which cluster about the concept
"art": (I) creation or execution of art works, (II) art
appreciation, and (III) critical talk about art. Activity
one, the execution or actual production of art objects, will
not suffice as a definition of aesthetics. Aesthetics does
not entail the doing or practice of art: painting, sculpting,
writing poetry, or the like. Of course, there are cases
in which an aesthetician's literary style is of genuine
artistic merit, but this is not his basic task. It is,
rather, the distinctive role of the artist to create or
produce art objects. If one distinguishes between the
adjective "aesthetic" meaning "artistic" and the noun
"aesthetics" referring to "a branch of philosophy," there
is little danger of confusing the activity of the gifted
artist with the technical study of the aesthetician.

As to the unbrella expression "art appreciation,"
while this may be a fringe benefit of the discipline called
aesthetics, increased pleasure in one's commerce with art or
enhanced enjoyment of art is peripheral not central to
inquiries into aesthetics. Art appreciation is definitely
not the major goal of the aesthetician. Such an enrichment

of one's encounters with art, if precipitated by a study of aesthetics, is only an extra reward. The specific attempt to familiarize individuals with actual art works and to inculcate the relevant sensitivities is usually deemed to be within the province of an art department. As John Hospers has noted,[1] art appreciation may be silent, but whatever else aesthetics is, it is not silent. If aesthetics is not to be identified with the doing or savoring of art, what other sort of activity might be mistaken for aesthetics?

By the expression "critical talk about art" I mean the critical remarks of laymen, artists, and especially professional critics. Critical talk or criticism, contrary to popular opinion, need not be negative in tone; criticism simply means judgment as to how a work is best described, interpreted, or evaluated. Although critical talk about individual works may be a means to doing aesthetics, it is not the substance of aesthetics. Discussions of specific works of art belong more squarely in the domain of art criticism. When one attempts to (a) describe, (b) interpret, or (c) evaluate particular works of art, he is functioning mainly in

[1] Introductory Readings in Aesthetics, ed. John Hospers (New York: Collier-Macmillan, 1969), p. 2.

the capacity of an art critic. Thus, the aesthetician who
elects to speak about the features of specific works tends to
be in the zone of art criticism, not the realm of aesthetics.
All such discussions of particular works will, however, not
be goals or ends in themselves for the aesthetician as
aesthetician. Instead, they will be the means by which he
obtains information which is pertinent to aesthetics itself.

Having surveyed the creation of art, art appreciation,
and art criticism and having found that none of these activities
is to be equated with aesthetics, we now turn to a more direct
characterization of aesthetics as double-talk. Aesthetics can
be regarded as double-talk in that it is <u>critical talk about
critical talk about art</u>. Aesthetics critically analyzes the
critical remarks which people make about art. Why comment
upon the statments others have made concerning art? One may
do so in order to: (1) clarify the meaning of such statments
when necessary, (2) discover their truth or falsity, or (3)
determine their theoretical implications. To what theories
do they point? What philosophical questions do they raise?
Let us see how each of these three cases can be illustrated.
For an example of case (1), consider the aesthetician who might

4

ask of the art critic: "What exactly do you mean when you use the term 'creativity'? Is 'creativity' tantamount to mere novelty? Is producing something which is different a sufficient condition for producing a creative object?" The aesthetician may then argue that novelty is a necessary but not a sufficient condition for being a creative work. In short, he might maintain that an object must not only be different but also significant if it is to be deserving of the epithet "creative," the latter being a term with nuances of praise. Thus, an aesthetician might conclude that creativity requires not mere novelty, but significant novelty. By "significant" I mean "worthy of attention"--witty, eye-appealing, informative, insightful, emotionally moving, and so on. Obviously, significance would be context-dependent. Perhaps the point is clear, however, that creativity is not predicable of that which is only novel, unusual, weird, or different.

For an example of case (2), consider the following claim from a recent textbook on painting: "A good drawing or painting must project a deeply felt mood." The aesthetician would be apt to ask: "Is this assertion true?" Is it really a fact that all good drawings and paintings do communicate some intensely felt emotional quality? Reflection may convince the aesthetician that this is false. An abstract painting, which does not convey any distinctive emotion or emotional ambience, could be cited as a counter-example, provided that it is judged worthwhile on some other grounds. It may possess an intriguing design or exhibit a delicacy of brush strokes.

For an instance of (3), suppose an aesthetician examines the following quotation from Chaiman Mao Tse-tung:

> (Our purpose is) to ensure that literature and art fit well into the whole revolutionary machine as a component part, that they operate as powerful weapons for uniting and educating the people and for attacking and destroying the enemy, and that they help the people fight the enemy with one heart and one mind. [2]

What theory of art is implicit in or suggested by such remarks? Statements of this kind point to a theory known as instrumentalism. This outlook holds that art or good art is that which accomplishes some practical goal; some definite purpose must be served. Here, the orientation is decidely pragmatic, since art is regarded as an instrument or tool. The aesthetician will note that instrumentalism raises the philosophical question: What is the relationship between form and content in a work of art? Related questions include: Should not art

---

[2] Quotations from Chairman Mao Tse-tung, Introduction by A. Doak Barnett (New York: Bantam Books, Inc., 1967), p. 173.

works be evaluated in terms of such formal categories as line, shape, rhythm, color arrangements and the like? Should not one focus upon intrinsic features (properties inherent in the work itself) and ignore what is extrinsic, namely any social-political impact or consequences? Those who advocate exclusive concentration upon formal aspects are defending a theory which is aptly called "formalism." Thus, the aesthetician is often involved in articulating theoretical considerations and philosophical questions which are embedded in the comments that men make about art. Aesthetics, therefore, tends to be more rarified or abstract than, for example, art criticism. Consider the movement from concreteness to increasing abstraction that is illustrated in the following, admittedly oversimplified, sequence. Suppose we look for greater and greater conceptualization by focusing upon the painting "Night Hawks" by the American realist Edward Hopper. (1) In the activity of painting or producing this particular work, Hopper wielded concrete materials in order to produce a concrete product. (2) In the activity of art appreciation, one might climax his examination of Hopper's work by labeling the painting "powerful". Powerful is a concept, an abstraction. Conceptualization was needed in order to arrive at this label. In the activity of painting, no matter how conceptual the process, a physical product is a necessary consequence; in the case of art appreciation, only abstract thought or conceptualization is produced, for the physical product has already been created. (3) Now consider the activity of the art critic who seeks to explain such powerfulness through further abstractions: "Naturally the picture is powerful, since it succeeds in stirring a familiar emotion. The deserted, late night or early morning street, the harsh artificial light of the diner, the figure with his back to us--all suggest the existential aloneness or alienation which can accompany urban existence, even when one finds himself in a crowd. There is a poignant quality which any city dweller can sense." (4) Finally, the aesthetician is perhaps best understood as one who engages in critical reflection upon the critical reflections of the art critic. The aesthetician might ask: What theory of art do the art critic's view imply? A certain mood, ambience, or emotional tone is said to be conveyed by the painting. In other words, the work is judged

8

successful because it effectively transmits human emotion. The theory of art can be identified as the communication theory. The aesthetician might then proceed to ask if transmitting emotion is a necessary condition for good art. The degree of abstraction which characterizes the aesthetician's activities is illustrated by the fact that he need not necessarily always have a first hand acquaintance with the work which is under discussion. In other words, there are times when the aesthetician can clarify the language of an art critic, discover something as to the truth or falsity of his remarks (Are they coherent or consistent with each other?), and pinpoint the theoretical import of the critic's utterances, all without having confronted the work to which the critic's remarks are directed.

What, then is aesthetics? It is double-talk or critical reflection upon critical reflections upon art. For this reason, aesthetics is sometimes referred to as <u>criticism of criticism</u> or <u>meta-criticism</u>. Aesthetics as double-talk involves critically analyzing critical statements concerning art for the purpose of clarifying such statements, discovering their truth or falsity, or determining their theoretical ramifications. Aesthetics is not, however, limited to double-talk or criticism of criticism. Were this the case, aesthetics would be entirely parasitic on the critical comments of nonaestheticians--except, of course, for those times when the aesthetician critically analyzes his own art-related notions. Aesthetics is what aestheticians do and this includes the framing of theories of art. Aestheticians sometimes formulate or conjure up a theory of art. Rather than call aesthetics an activity, as Wittgenstein does philosophy itself, aesthetics is best described as a set of activities consisting of meta-criticism, theory construction, or any combination of the two. The aesthetician may, for example, critically analyze a theory of art and, in so doing, develop an alternative theory as a response. Clearly not all critical analyses of theories or critical remarks will eventuate in the development of a new theory. But aesthetics remains distinctly theoretical. The aesthetician is either con-structing theories of art, critically analyzing theories of art, or critically analyzing statements which imply theories of art.

10

WHAT IS AN AESTHETIC EXPERIENCE?

"What kind of an experience is an aesthetic experience?" is somewhat like the question: "Have you stopped beating your wife?" Both questions carry implicit suggestions. The second may be incorrect in suggesting that one has ever beaten his wife; the first may incorrectly suggest that there is only one kind of aesthetic experience. The title of the present work, Varieties of Aesthetic Experience, denies any such homogeneity of aesthetic experiences just as did William James' classic The Varieties of Religious Experience with respect to religious experiences. That everything from a sunset to a urinal has been thematic in aesthetic experience suggests that any object can serve as the basis for an aesthetic experience. Granted that anything can be the object of an aesthetic experience, would we not expect variations from one such experience to another? The literature of aesthetics is replete with examples which demonstrate the great variety which obtains among aesthetic experiences; some are intensely emotional, others relatively detached; some are pervaded by feelings of the sublime, others

11

by feelings of the ridiculous. Nevertheless, it can still make sense to seek one or more common denominators which link the various kinds. Considering the homely orange, while there are Valencia, Temple, and other varieties of oranges, defining characteristics which are common to all of them can be specified: some sweetness of taste, the presence of citric acid, roundish shape, and rather like coloration. Three unifying earmarks or defining traits of aesthetic experiences can be identified.

First one can recognize a trans-practical quality. Reading the novel War and Peace, viewing the film "Citizen Kane", and studying Michelangelo's "David" all demand non-practical appreciation if the art works are to be aesthetically experienced. This is not to say that trans-practical appreciation cannot coexist or alternate with practical appreciation. Insofar as one's valuation is not exclusively practical, aesthetic experience becomes possible. Suppose that one decides to read War and Peace for the practical purpose of writing a book report. This does not preclude the reader from deriving non-practical satisfaction from his enterprise. Such non-practical

12

appreciation may be called aesthetic. In short, the novel is being appreciated aesthetically to the extent that it is being savored for its own sake, as an end in itself, or as intrinsically rewarding rather than as only a means to some other end such as composing a book report. To the degree that one apprehends data sheerly for the rewards which are provided by that apprehension alone, an experience is aesthetic.

Thus, a given experience may contain practical and non-practical qualities. But it is by virtue of the latter that the experience is an aesthetic experience. Actually, there are three possibilities. In what might be called a wholly aesthetic experience, the satisfaction derived is exclusively non-practical as, for instance, in the contemplation of an abstract painting which one finds to be engrossing yet devoid of practical relevance. In a mixed aesthetic experience, non-practical and practical factors are present simultaneously and may be inseparable. For example, one may be unable to separate the aesthetic satisfaction produced by the eye-appealing shape of an airplance from the practical satisfaction produced by the

13

knowledge that this shape is aerodynamically efficient and would contribute to great speed. These first two cases correspond to Kant's distinction between free and dependent beauty. Finally, there are cases in which one oscillates between aesthetic and practical appreciation. Reading a passage from War and Peace, one might first appreciate its evocative power and then its appropriateness for quotation in a book report. Considering our orange again, one might first concentrate upon its interesting pebble-covered surface; next, one might view and value it entirely for its practical merit as source of vitamin C. An aesthetic experience is, therefore, never completely practical in character; one appreciates an object, to some extent at least, for its own inherent significance or meaningfulness.

Frequently, it is a non-practical feature of an object which initiates an aesthetic experience. Suppose that one attends to the ornate flourishes which decorate the handle of a spoon. Perceiving these inessential curves for their own visually satisfying qualities is a case of aesthetically experiencing the spoon. Of course, the same spoon could

14

be an aesthetic success owing to its decorative properties and a practical failure due to its shallow depression being ill-equipped to hold an adequate amount of food. But the matter is more complex than the above illustration would suggest, for if any object can be thematic in aesthetic experience, then something as functional and "frill-free" as a wooden lead pencil can serve as the subject for an aesthetic experience. One may become fascinated by it as a vivid band of color or a stream-lined form--whether or not its lead is of the right diameter for the purpose at hand. Here many adults could learn from the child who is delighted on receiving a first pencil. Part of the child's satisfaction is undoubtedly aesthetic; he has not yet become preoccupied with the practical con-cerns which can extinguish aesthetic sensitivity and enjoyment.

A trans-mundane quality is a second characteristic of aesthetic experiences. This means that an aesthetic experience is phenomenologically outstanding; it stands out or apart from the usually undifferentiated continuum of humdrum experiences, the welter of ordinary experiences.

15

Aesthetic experience, like religious experience, marks a break from the prosaic, a departure from the commonplace. It is, then, something extraordinary. Of course, in the chemistry of an aesthetic experience, the most ordinary objects can become transformed into extraordinary entities-- a simple leaf, for instance, may become the matrix from which a highly complex, vein-created pattern emerges. One's interpretation of the data determines whether the trans-mundane experience is regarded as religious or naturalistic in character. If one is religiously disposed, he may be inclined to attach religious significance to the experience. An atheist, on the other hand, could interpret even a vision of the divine naturalistically as the fanciful product of educational brainwashing coupled with, say, wish-fulfillment.

Finally, one can detect a trans-chaotic quality in aesthetic experiences. There is something integrated, unified, organized, or coherent about an aesthetic experience; the phases or parts which make up the said experience merge, blend, fuse, coalesce, or stand in some clear relationship to each other. Such an experience has a focus, a clarity, a distinctness that separates it from the blurry components which constitute everyday experiences. This trans-chaotic or unified feature is closely related to the trans-mundane quality inasmuch as a high degree of unity contributes to the uncommon nature of aesthetic experiences. Ordinarily, the ingredients which compose an experience are connected only objectively, as it were, by virtue of proximity in space, or by virtue of simultaneity or succession in time, but they are not apprehended consciously or subjectively as linked or productive of a whole.

A word must be added concerning the unity of aesthetic experiences. We can distinguish between sequential and non-sequential unity. In the first case, there is unity of progression or continuity. Consider the scenes of a play which are unified by an uninterrupted momentum and movement that eventuates in a consummation, a fulfilling conclusion. Dialogue, events, and scenes succeed each other in a natural, satisfying way. Unity of continuity is sequential, since the well-integrated elements will not so fit together in any arbitrary sequence. Non-sequential unity might be dubbed the unity of equillibrium or stasis.

17

Imagine a Persian rug in which one color balances another, one shape complements another, and one line harmonizes with another. Objective unities possessed by art works naturally generate an awareness or general impression of unity in the spectator. Thus, the overall experience is qualified by apprehension of a degree of integration which far exceeds that of so-called normal experiences. Earlier we discussed a nonsequential aesthetic experience of a pencil; now let us consider a sequential aesthetic experience of the same pencil. Usually, the steps which make up the process of sharpening a pencil run together and are not differentiated. But one may first look at the dull pencil point, then watch the fireworks of wood shavings and the evolving point as the pencil sharpener is turned, and finally study the end result--a needle sharp point. Such a little drama has a beginning, middle, and end. Of course, to say that anything can be the object of an aesthetic experience is not to say that all things are equally deserving of our attention; an actual fireworks display would probably be more rewarding than the pyrotechnics produced by sharpening a pencil.

To sum up, whenever an experience is characterized by trans-practical appreciation, trans-mundane significance, and trans-chaotic structure, it is an aesthetic experience. Unity and the extraordinary may both be present in a non-aesthetic experience, but only the presence of trans-practical appreciation insures that the experience is aesthetic. Being robbed at gun point may be a highly unified experience and, given the best of lives, it is certainly out of the ordinary, but it is not likely to be an aesthetic experience, for only the masochist or arch-esthete is apt to engage in trans-practical appreciation during the encounter.

In the selections which follow, seven authors provide suggestions for an answer to our leading question: What is an aesthetic experience? These seven readings are sometimes complementary and sometimes at odds with each other, but, most importantly, each writer has proven himself able to stimulate reflection on the nature of aesthetic experience. The reader is encouraged to weigh the various accounts against each other and against the account which I have presented in order to reach his or her own conclusions.

19

AESTHETIC EXPERIENCE AS DREAM-LIKE

The following excerpt from Jean-Paul Sartre's <u>Psychology of the</u>
<u>Imagination</u>, while concerned with the existential status of the
work of art, at the same time, sketches out what he takes
to be the dynamics of aesthetic experience. Early in his
remarks, he labels the art work an unreality. The essay
continues by explaining that the imagination is responsible
for the creation of such unrealities. Imagination itself
is a kind of consciousness. Thus, Sartre speaks of the person
who is having an aesthetic experience as performing an
"intentional act of an imaginative consciousness." In his
words, " . . . the spectator assumes the imaginative attitude
. . . . " Aesthetic experience occurs when one's imaginative
consciousness conjures up, as it were, unreal entities. Real
objects act as catalysts, springboards, or stimuli for the
production of aesthetic objects which are always unreal. To
have an aesthetic experience, then, is to enter a realm of
unreal objects and events: "Esthetic contemplation is an
induced dream and the passing into the real is an actual
waking up."

For Sartre, aesthetic experiences are trans-mundane, not only in our sense of being uncommon or extraordinary, but in the much stronger sense of involving concentration upon that which is "out of the world." "The nauseating disgust that characterizes the consciousness of reality," a theme which is developed at length in Sartre's novel Nausea, squares with his conviction that the "'beautiful' . . . is out of the world." Aesthetic experience takes place only if consciousness becomes imaginative and the objects of the world are negated. One negates or denies real objects in order to posit imaginative substitutes. A spectator who sees Sir Laurence Olivier perform as Hamlet must deny the real person Olivier in order to dwell in the unreal domain of Hamlet and thereby aesthetically experience the drama.

Since his emphasis is upon the trans-mundane, Sartre makes only passing reference to the trans-chaotic quality of aesthetic experience in the expressions "unreal synthetic whole" and "unreal whole." We find one allusion to the trans-practical aspect of aesthetic experiences in Sartre's warning that one should not mistake the moral for the

22

aesthetic: ". . . it is stupid to confuse the moral with
the aesthetic. The values of the Good presume being-in-
the-world, they concern action in the real . . ." Phrased
differently, the moral sphere, unlike the aesthetic,
necessarily calls for practical engagement or involvement
in the real world.

Sartre's contention that aesthetic experience begins
only when perception of the real is superseded by imagination
of the unreal raises the question: What is the relationship
between art and reality? An opponent might ask: Cannot a
case of sensitive perception of the real ever constitute a
case of aesthetic experience? Finally, from among the
numerous questions posed by Sartre's analysis, one might
inquire as to whether or not Sartre gives sufficient grounds
for excluding isolated sensuous enjoyments from the category
of the aesthetic.

THE WORK OF ART

"It is not our intention to deal here with the problem of the
work of art in its entirety. Closely related as this problem
is to the question of the Imaginary, its treatment calls
for a special work in itself. But it is time we drew some
conclusions from the long investigations in which we used
as an example a statue or the portrait of Charles VIII or
a novel. The following comments will be concerned essentially
with the existential type of the work of art. And we can
at once formulate the law that the work of art is an unreality.

This appeared to us clearly from the moment we took for
our example, in an entirely different connection, the portrait
of Charles VIII. We understood at the very outset that this
Charles VIII was an object. But this, obviously, is not the
same object as is the painting, the canvas, which are the
real objects of the painting. As long as we observe the
canvas and the frame for themselves the esthetic object
'Charles VIII' will not appear. It is not that it is hidden
by the picture, but because it cannot present itself to a
realizing consciousness. It will appear at the moment when

consciousness, undergoing a radical change in which the world is negated, will itself become imaginative. The situation here is like that of the cubes which can be seen at will to be five or six in number. It will not do to say that when they are seen as five it is because at that time the aspect of the drawing in which they are six is <u>concealed.</u> The intentional act that apprehends them as five is sufficient unto itself, it is complete and <u>exclusive</u> of the act which grasps them as six. And so it is with the apprehension of Charles VIII as an image which is depicted on the picture. This Charles VIII on the canvas is necessarily the correlative of the intentional act of an imaginative consciousness. And since this Charles VIII, who is an unreality so long as he is grasped on the canvas, is precisely the object of our esthetic appreciations (it is he who 'moves' us, who is 'painted with intelligence, power, and grace,' etc.), we are led to recognize that, in a picture, the esthetic object is something <u>unreal</u>. This is of great enough importance once we remind ourselves of the way in which we ordinarily confuse the real and the imaginary in a work of art. We often hear it said, in fact, that the artist first has an idea in the

form of an image which he then _realizes_ on canvas. This
mistaken notion arises from the fact that the painter can,
in fact, begin with a mental image which is, as such,
incommunicable, and from the fact that at the end of his
labors he presents the public with an object which anyone
can observe. This leads us to believe that there occurred
a transition from the imaginary to the real. But this is
in no way true. That which is real, we must not fail to
note, are the results of the brush strokes, the stickiness
of the canvas, its grain, the polish spread over the colors.
But all this does not constitute the object of esthetic
appreciation. What is 'beautiful' is something which cannot
be experienced as a perception and which, by its very nature,
is out of the world. We have just shown that it cannot be
brightened, for instance, by projecting a light beam on the
canvas: it is the canvas that is brightened and not the
painting. The fact of the matter is that the painter did
not _realize_ his mental image at all: he has simply constructed
a material analogue of such a kind that everyone can grasp the
image provided he looks at the analogue. But the image
thus provided with an external analogue remains an image.

26

There is no realization of the imaginary, nor can we speak of its objectification. Each stroke of the brush was not made for itself nor even for the constructing of a coherent real whole (in the sense in which it can be said that a certain lever in a machine was conceived in the interest of the whole and not for itself). It was given together with an unreal synthetic whole and the aim of the artist was to construct a whole of real colors which enable this unreal to manifest itself. The painting should then be conceived as a material thing visited from time to time (every time that the spectator assumes the imaginative attitude) by an unreal which is precisely the painted object. What deceives us here is the real and sensuous pleasure which certain real colors on the canvas give us. Some reds of Matisse, for instance, produce a sensuous enjoyment in those who see them. But we must understand that this sensuous enjoyment, if thought of in isolation - for instance, if aroused by a color in nature - has nothing of the esthetic. It is purely and simply a pleasure of sense. But when the red of the painting is grasped, it is grasped in spite of every-

27

thing, as a part of an unreal whole and it is in this whole that it is beautiful. For instance it is the red of a rug by a table. There is, in fact, no such thing as pure color. Even if the artist is concerned solely with the sensory relationships between forms and colors, he chooses for that very reason a rug in order to increase the sensory value of the red: tactile elements, for instance, must be intended through the red, it is a fleecy red, because the rug is of a fleecy material. Without this 'fleeciness' of the color something would be lost. And surely the rug is painted there for the red it justifies and not the red for the rug. If Matisse chose a rug rather than a sheet of dry and glossy paper it is because of the voluptuous mixture of the color, the density and the tactile quality of the wool. Consequently the red can be truly enjoyed only in grasping it as the red of the rug, and therefore unreal. And he would have lost his strongest contrast with the green of the wall if the green were not rigid and cold, because it is the green of a wall tapestry. It is therefore in the unreal that the relationship of colors and forms takes on its real meaning. And even when

28

drawn objects have their usual meaning reduced to a minimum, as in the painting of the cubists, the painting is at least not flat. The forms we see are certainly not the forms of a rug, a table, nor anything else we see in the world. They nevertheless do have a density, a material, a depth, they bear a relationship of perspective towards each other. They are things. And it is precisely in the measure in which they are things that they are unreal. Cubism has introduced the fashion of claiming that a painting should not represent or imitate reality but should constitute an object in itself. As an aesthetic doctrine such a program is perfectly defensible and we owe many masterpieces to it. But it needs to be understood. To maintain that the painting, although altogether devoid of meaning, nevertheless is a real object, would be a grave mistake. It is certainly not an object of nature. The real object no longer functions as an analogue of a bouquet of flowers or a glade. But when I 'contemplate' it, I nevertheless am not in a realistic attitude. The painting is still an analogue. Only what manifests itself through it is an unreal collection of new things, of objects I have never seen or ever will see, but

which are not less unreal because of it, objects which do
not exist in the painting, nor anywhere in the world, but
which manifest themselves by means of the canvas, and which
have gotten hold of it by some sort of possession. And
it is the configuration of these unreal objects that I
designate as beautiful. The esthetic enjoyment is real
but it is not grasped for itself, as if produced by a real
color: it is but a manner of apprehending the unreal
object and, far from being directed on the real painting,
it serves to constitute the imaginary object through the
real canvas. This is the source of the celebrated
disinterestedness of esthetic experience. This is why
Kant was able to say that it does not matter whether the
object of beauty, when experienced as beautiful, is or is
not objectively real; why Schopenhauer was able to speak
of a sort of suspension of the Will. This does not come
from some mysterious way of apprehending the real, which
we are able to use occasionally. What happens is that
the esthetic object is constituted and apprehended by an
imaginative consciousness which posits it as unreal.

What we have just shown regarding painting is readily

30

applied to the art of fiction, poetry and drama, as well. It is self-evident that the novelist, the poet and the dramatist construct an unreal object by means of verbal analogues; it is also self-evident that the actor who plays Hamlet makes use of himself, of his whole body, as an analogue of the imaginary person. Even the famous dispute about the paradox of the comedian is enlightened by the view here presented. It is well known that certain amateurs proclaim that the actor <u>does not believe</u> in the character he portrays. Others, leaning on many witnesses, claim that the actor becomes identified in some way with the character he is enacting. To us these two views are not exclusive of each other; if by 'belief' is meant actually real it is obvious that the actor does not actually consider himself to be Hamlet. But this does not mean that he does not 'mobilize' all his powers to make Hamlet real. He uses all his feelings, all his strength, all his gestures as analogues of the feelings and conduct of Hamlet. But by this very fact he takes the reality away from them. <u>He lives completely in an unreal way</u>. And it matters little that he is <u>actually</u> weeping in enacting the role. These

31

tears, whose origin we explained above (See Part III, Chapter II) he himself experiences - and so does the audience - as the tears of Hamlet, that is as the analogue of unreal tears. The transformation that occurs here is like that we discussed in the dream: the actor is completely caught up, inspired, by the unreal. It is not the character who becomes real in the actor, it is the actor who becomes unreal in his character. [2]

But are there not some arts whose objects seem to escape unreality by their very nature? A melody, for instance, refers to nothing but itself. Is a cathedral anything more than a mass of real stone which dominates the surrounding house tops? But let us look at this matter more closely. I listen to a symphony orchestra, for instance, playing the Beethoven Seventh Symphony. Let us disregard exceptional cases - which are besides on the margin of aesthetic contemplation -

------

[2] It is in this sense that a beginner in the theatre can say that stage-fright served her to represent the timidity of Ophelia. If it did so, it is because she suddenly turned it into an unreality, that is, that she ceased to apprehend it for itself and that she grasped it as analogue for the timidity of Ophelia.

as when I go mainly 'to hear Toscanini' interpret Beethoven in his own way. As a general rule what draws me to the concert is the desire 'to hear the Seventh Symphony.' Of course I have some objection to hearing an amateur orchestra, and prefer this or that well-known musical organization. But this is due to my desire to hear the symphony 'played perfectly,' because the symphony will then be perfectly itself. The shortcomings of a poor orchestra which plays 'too fast' or 'too slow,' 'in the wrong tempo,' etc., seem to me to rob, to 'betray' the work it is playing. At most the orchestra effaces itself before the work it performs, and, provided I have reasons to trust the performers and their conductor, I am confronted by the symphony itself. This everyone will grant me. But now, what is the Seventh Symphony itself? Obviously it is a thing, that is something which is before me, which endures, which lasts. Naturally there is no need to show that that thing is a synthetic whole, which does not consist of tones but of a thematic configuration. But is that 'thing' real or unreal? Let us first bear in mind that I am listening to the Seventh Symphony. For me that 'Seventh Symphony' does not exist in time, I do not grasp it as a dated event, as an artistic manifestation which is unrolling itself in the Chatelet auditorium on the 17th of November, 1938. If I hear Furtwaengler tomorrow or eight days later conduct another orchestra performing the same symphony, I am in the presence of the same symphony once more. Only it is being played either better or worse. Let us now see how I hear the symphony: some persons shut their eyes. In this case they detach themselves from the visual and dated event of this particular interpretation: they give themselves up to the pure sounds. Others watch the orchestra or the back of the conductor. But they do not see what they are looking at. This is what Revault d'Allonnes calls reflection with auxiliary fascination. The auditorium, the conductor and even the orchestra have disappeared. I am therefore confronted by the Seventh Symphony, but on the express condition of understanding nothing about it, that I do not think of the event as an actuality and dated, and on condition that I listen to the succession of themes as an absolute succession and not as a real succession which is unfolding itself, for instance, on the occasion when Peter

34

paid a visit to this or that friend. In the degree to which I hear the symphony it is not here, between these walls, at the tip of the violin bows. Nor is it 'in the past' as if I thought: this is the work that matured in the mind of Beethoven on such a date. It is completely beyond the real. It has its own time, that is, it possesses an inner time, which runs from the first tone of the allegro to the last tone of the finale, but this time is not a succession of a preceding time which it continues and which happened 'before' the beginning of the allegro; nor is it followed by a time which will come 'after' the finale. The Seventh Symphony is in no way in time. It is therefore in no way real. It occurs by itself, but as absent, as being out of reach. I cannot act upon it, change a single note of it, or slow down its movement. But it depends on the real for its appearance: that the conductor does not faint away, that a fire in the hall does not put an end to the performance. From this we cannot conclude that the Seventh Symphony has come to an end. No, we only think that the performance of the symphony has ceased. Does this not show clearly that the performance of the symphony is its analogue? It can manifest itself only through analogues which are dated and which unroll in our time. But to experience it on these analogues the imaginative reduction must be functioning, that is, the real sounds must be apprehended as analogues. It therefore occurs as a perpetual elsewhere, a perpetual absence. We must not picture it (as does Spandrell in Point Counterpoint by Huxley - as so many platonisms) as existing in another world, in an intelligible heaven. It is not only outside of time and space - as are essences, for instance - it is outside of the real, outside of existence. I do not hear it actually, I listen to it in the imaginary. Here we find the explanation for the considerable difficulty we always experience in passing from the world of the theatre or of music into that of our daily affairs. There is in fact no passing from one world into the other, but only a passing from the imaginative attitude to that of reality. Esthetic contemplation is an induced dream and the passing into the real is an actual waking up. We often speak of the 'deception' experienced on returning to reality. But this does not explain that this discomfort also exists, for instance, after having witnessed a realistic and cruel play, in which case reality should be experienced as comforting. This discomfort is simply that of the dreamer on awakening; an entranced consciousness, engulfed in the imaginary, is suddenly freed by the sudden ending of the play, of the symphony, and comes suddenly in contact with existence. Nothing more is needed to arouse the nauseating disgust that characterizes the consciousness of reality.

From these few observations we can already conclude that the real is never beautiful. Beauty is a value applicable only to the imaginary and which means the negation of the world in its essential structure. This is why it is stupid to confuse the moral with the esthetic. The values of the Good presume being-in-the-world, they concern action in the real and are subject from the outset to the basic absurdity of existence. To say that we 'assume' an esthetic attitude to life is to constantly confuse the real and the imaginary. It does happen, however, that we do assume the attitude of esthetic contemplation towards real events or objects. But in such cases everyone of us can feel in himself a sort of recoil in relation to the object contemplated which slips

37

into nothingness so that, from this moment on, it is no longer
perceived; it fuctions as an analogue of itself, that is,
that an unreal image of what it is appears to us through
its actual presence. This image can be purely and simply
the object 'itself' neutralized, annihilated as when I
contemplate a beautiful woman or death at a bull fight;
it can also be the imperfect and confused appearance of
what it could be through what it is, as when the painter
grasps the harmony of two colors as being greater, more
vivid, through the real blots he finds on a wall. The
object at once appears to be in back of itself, becomes
untouchable, it is beyond our reach; and hence arises a
sort of sad disinterest in it. It is in this sense that
we may say that great beauty in a woman kills the desire
for her. In fact we cannot at the same time place ourselves
on the plane of the esthetic when this unreal 'herself'
which we admire appears and on the realistic plane of
physical possession. To desire her we must forget she is
beautiful, because desire is a plunge into the heart of
existence, into what is most contingent and most absurd.
Esthetic contemplation of real objects is of the same

structure as paramnesia, in which the real object functions as analogue of itself in the past. But in one of the cases there is a negating and in the other a placing a thing in the past. Paramnesia differs from the esthetic attitude as memory differs from imagination."

AESTHETIC EXPERIENCE AS A THREE-FOLD PHENOMENON

Beardsley's clear and compact discussion of the components in aesthetic experience singles out unity, intensity, and complexity as features common to such experiences. What he describes as unity corresponds to what we have called the trans-chaotic or integrated quality. What he characterizes as intensity is related to, but not identical with, what we have termed the trans-mundane dimension of aesthetic experiences. His third trait, complexity, brings up the question of whether or not one can have an aesthetic experience of a single sound or a single patch of color which is larger than one's visual field. Beardsley's emphasis upon sensuous presentations and the perceptual may prompt one to ask if this theory can accomodate so-called conceptual art. In a brief comment, Beardsley acknowledges the trans-practical status of aesthetic experiences, for he speaks of the absence of ". . . any necessary commitment to practical action, that is characteristic of aesthetic experience."

AESTHETIC EXPERIENCE

"The problem is whether we can isolate, and describe in general terms, certain features of experience that are peculiarly characteristic of our intercourse with aesthetic objects. Of course, listening to music is a very different experience in some ways from looking through a cathedral or watching a motion picture. Reading literature certainly does something to us, and probably _for_ us, that listening to music cannot do, and vice versa. A full account of our experience of aesthetic objects would have to deal carefully with these matters. But is there something that all these experiences have in common-something that can be usefully distinguished? This is at least an empirical question, open to inquiry. And some inquiry has been made, though many mysteries remain. However, we can be reasonably confident of certain generalizations, which some writers have obtained by acute introspection, and which each of us can test in his own experience. [2]

---

[2] In the following pages, supplemented by further remarks in Note 28-B, I rely most heavily upon the work of John Dewey, Edward Bullough, I.A. Richards, and Immanuel Kant; for references see Note 28-B.

These are the points on which, I take it, nearly everyone will agree:

First, an aesthetic experience is one in which attention is firmly fixed upon heterogeneous but interrelated components of a phenomenally objective field-visual or auditory patterns, or the characters and events in literature. Some writers have suggested that in such an experience, as when we are deeply absorbed in the tension of a visual design or in the developing design of music, the distinction between phenomenal objectivity and phenomenal subjectivity itself tends to disappear. This may be overstated, but in any case the experience differs from the loose play of fancy in daydreaming by having a central focus; the eye is kept on the object, and the object controls the experience. It is all right, I think, to speak of the object as causing the experience, but of course the connection is more intimate, for the object, which is a perceptual object, also appears in the experience as its phenomenally objective field.

Second, it is an experience of some intensity. Some writers have said that it is an experience pervasively dominated by intense feeling or emotion, but these terms still occupy a dubious position in psychological theory; what we call the emotion in an aesthetic experience may be simply the intensity of the experience itself. In any case, the emotion is characteristically bound to its object, the phenomenal field itself - we feel sad about the characters, or uncertain about the results of an unexpected modulation. Aesthetic objects give us a concentration of experience. The drama presents only, so to speak, a segment of human life, that part of it that is noteworthy and significant, and fixes our minds on that part; the painting and the music invite us to do what we would seldom do in ordinary life - pay attention only to what we are seeing or hearing, and ignore everything else. They summon up our energies for an unusually narrow field of concern. Large-scale novels may do more; they are in fact always in danger of dissipating attention by spreading it out into our usual diffuse awareness of the environment.

This is why the expression 'feeling no pain' is particularly apt to aesthetic experience. The pleasure

44

is not often comparable in intensity to the pleasures of satisfying the ordinary appetites. But the concentration of the experience can shut out all the negative responses - the trivial distracting noises, organic disturbances, thoughts of unpaid bills and unwritten letters and unpurged embarrassments - that so often clutter up our pleasures. It does what whiskey does, only not by dulling sensitivity and clouding the awareness, but by marshalling the attention for a time into free and unobstructed channels of experience.

But this discussion already anticipates the two other features of aesthetic experience, which may both be subsumed under unity. For, third, it is an experience that hangs together, or is coherent, to an unusually high degree. One thing leads to another; continuity of development, without gaps or dead spaces, a sense of overall providential pattern of guidance, an orderly cumulation of energy toward a climax, are present to an unusual degree. Even when the experience is temporarily broken off, as when we lay down the novel to water the lawn or eat dinner, it can retain a remarkable degree of coherence. Pick up the novel and you are immediately back in the world of the work, almost as if there had been

45

no interruption. Stop the music because of a mechanical problem, or the ringing of a phone, but when it is started again, two bars may be enough to establish the connection with what went before, and you are clearly in the <u>same</u> experience again.

Fourth, it is an experience that is unusually complete in itself. The impulses and expectations aroused by elements within the experience are felt to be counterbalanced or resolved by other elements within the experience, so that some degree of equilibrium or finality is achieved and enjoyed. The experience detaches itself, and even insulates itself, from the intrusion of alien elements. Of course, it cannot survive all emergencies. I have heard the last movement of Beethoven's '<u>Waldstein</u>' <u>Sonata</u> (<u>Op</u>. <u>53</u>) interrupted by a fire chief who suddenly appeared on stage to clear the aisles of standees; and even though the pianist, Paul Badura-Skoda, started off again at the beginning of the movement, he could not, of course, recapture the peculiar quality of that beginning, which moves without pause from the slow section of the sonata. But because of the highly concentrated, or localized, attention characteristic of aesthetic experience,

46

it tends to mark itself out from the general stream of experience, and stand in memory as a single experience.

Aesthetic objects have a peculiar, but I think important, aspect: they are all, so to speak, objects manques. There is something lacking in them that keeps them from being quite real, from achieving the full status of things - or, better, that prevents the question of reality from arising. They are complexes of qualities, surfaces. The characters of the novel or lyric have truncated histories, they are no more than they show. The music is movement without anything solid that moves; the object in the painting is not a material object, but only the appearance of one. Even the lifelike statue, though it gives us the shape and gesture and life of a living thing, is clearly not one itself. And the dancer gives us the abstractions of human action - the gestures and movements of joy and sorrow, of love and fear - but not the actions (killing or dying) themselves. This is one sense of 'make-believe' in which aesthetic objects are make-believe objects; and upon this depends their capacity to call forth from us the kind of admiring contemplation, without any necessary commitment to practical

47

action, that is characteristic of aesthetic experience.

One aesthetic experience may differ from another in any or all of three connected but independent respects: (1) it may be more unified, that is, more coherent and/or complete, than the other; (2) its dominant quality, or pervasisve feeling-tone, may be more intense than that of the other; (3) the range or diversity of distinct elements that it brings together into its unity, and under its dominant quality, may be more complex than that of the other. It will be convenient to have a general term to cover all three characteristics. I propose to say that one aesthetic experience has a greater magnitude - that is, it is more of an aesthetic experience - than another; and that its magnitude is a function of a least these three variables. For the more unified the experience, the more of a whole the experience is, and the more concentratedly the self is engaged; the more intense the experience, the more deeply the self is engaged; . . . that is, the more wide-ranging are its responses, perhaps over a longer time.

I do not think of magnitude here as implying measurement - it is merely a collective term for how much is happening, intensively or extensively, in the experience. It may be too vague a concept to be useful. That remains to be seen, but there are two sources of legitimate uneasiness about it that should be frankly faced at once. First, note that I am now applying the terms 'unity,' 'complexity,' and 'intensity' more broadly than before - not only to the phenomenally objective presentations in the experience, but to the whole experience, which includes affective and cognitive elements as well. The terms are still understandable, even in this extended use, I judge, but of course less capable of sure and exact application. Second, though I claim that these three characteristics all have a bearing upon magnitude, and that the magnitude of the experience is a resultant of them, I am not yet raising certain questions - which will shortly come to our attention - concerning the comparability of magnitudes. Evidently it will be possible to say that of two experiences approximately equal in unity and complexity, the one having a greater intensity will have the greater magnitude. But what if they are equal in one respect, and differ in opposite ways in the other two? This question is still open.

49

The traits of aesthetic experience are to be found individually in a great many other experiences, of course, but not in the same combination, I think. Play, in the sense in which we play games, involves the enjoyment of activity that has no practical purpose. But though the psychology of play has not yielded up all its secrets to psychological inquiry, it seems not necessarily to be an experience of a high degree of unity. Watching a baseball or football game is also generally lacking in a dominant pattern and consummation, though sometimes it has these characteristics to a high degree and is an aesthetic experience. Carrying through a triumphant scientific investigation or the solution of a mathematical problem may have the clear dramatic pattern and consummatory conclusion of an aesthetic experience, but it is not itself aesthetic experience unless the movement of thought is tied closely to sensuous presentations, or at least a phenomenally objective field of perceptual objects.

Such distinctions are vague and tentative; they are some of the problems that most need to be studied at the present time. In any case, we can identify aesthetic

50

experience as a kind of experience, though it is unique

only in its combination of traits, rather than in any

specific one. And we can say that aesthetic objects,

generally speaking, have the function of producing such

experiences, even though quite often aesthetic experiences

of some degree of magnitude are obtained in the regular

course of life from other things than aesthetic objects.

This is their special use, what they are good for. On

the whole, it is what they do best; they do it most

dependably, and they alone do it in the highest magnitude."

AESTHETIC EXPERIENCE AS MENTAL DISTANCE

Bullough's article proposes the principle of "Psychical Distance" as a logical prerequisite for and a necessary feature of aesthetic experience. By this principle, he means that the essential characteristic of aesthetic consciousness is mental distance, as it were, between one's self and the object of attention. To attain psychical distance, one must mentally abstract from an experience its practical meanings or implications and focus instead upon the so-called objective properties of the phenomenon. This shift from an ordinary outlook to that of psychical distance is compared to a sudden illumination which gives fresh significance to one's perception of the most mundane objects. A trans-practical standpoint is called for in that one must disengage the phenomenon under consideration from his practical self. That Bullough regards aesthetic experience as trans-mundane is obvious from his claim that the distanced perspective is emphatically not one's ordinary outlook. Through the operation of psychical distance, the usually unobserved aspects of things are revealingly "spotlighted." Bullough touches upon the trans-chaotic

53

quality of aesthetic experience when he talks about the "unification of presentment" which marks off "the object from the confused, disjointed, and scattered forms of actual experience."

Bullough's thought-provoking essay gives rise to various questions and problems. One may begin by asking: Is distance an indispensable element in aesthetic experience? If distance necessarily implies duality, are there not aesthetic experiences of total absorbtion? Granted that judging or evaluating an experience entails a dualism between subject and object, is Bullough confusing having an experience with assessing it? Is not complete identification or, at least, oscillation between a distanced state and utter absorbtion sometimes a desirable aspect of aesthetic experiences? Put succinctly, is Bullough denying the possibility of monistic aesthetic experiences?

To say "practical interest snaps" is to use an extreme and misleading metaphor. The expression implies that there is an absolute dichotomy between aesthetic and practical interest and that the twain shall never meet. But, as we earlier noted, there are several possibilities. Practical

54

interest may be altogether absent from an aesthetic experience; in other cases, however, practical interest may co-exist or fuse with trans-practical interest; in still other instances, the two interests may rapidly alternate. In his fog example, Bullough himself admits that practical dimensions "may incidentally enter into the enjoyment and enhance it." Nevertheless, phrases like "the cutting-out of the practical side of things and our practical attitude toward them" may mistakenly suggest that there can be no case of the co-presence of aesthetic appreciation and practical engagement.

To find the truth lurking in Bullough's account, psychical distance must be reinterpreted. The distanced view of things must not be understood as a different way of viewing or seeing, as though through a filter, but as either the viewing or seeing of different things or the viewing or seeing of things from a different context. One concentrates upon what is relevant from an aesthetic context or horizon rather than from an exclusively practical stand-point.

PSYCHICAL DISTANCE

" I. 1. Meaning of the term 'Distance.'

    2. Distance as a factor in Art.

    3. Distance as an aesthetic principle.

II. 1. Distance describes a personal relation.

    2. The antinomy of Distance.

    3. The variability of Distance.

    4. ~~Distance as the psychological formulation of the~~
       anti-realism of Art: naturalistic and idealistic
       Art.

    5. Distance as applied to the antithesis 'sensual'
       and 'spiritual.'

    6. Distance as applied to the antithesis 'individualisti
       and 'typical.'

III. Distance as an aesthetic principle:

    1. as a criterion between the agreeable and the
       beautiful.

    2. as a phase of artistic production: falsity of the
       theory of 'self-expression of the artist.'

    3. Distance and some recent aesthetic theories.

4. Distance as a fundamental principle of the 'aesthetic consciousness.'

I.

1. The conception of 'Distance' suggests, in connexion with Art, certain trains of thought by no means devoid of interest or of speculative importance. Perhaps the most obvious suggestion is that of actual spatial distance, i.e. the distance of a work of Art from the spectator, or that of represented spatial distance, i.e. the distance represented within the work. Less obvious, more metaphorical, is the meaning of temporal distance. The first was noticed already by Aristotle in his Poetics; the second has played a great part in the history of painting in the form of perspective; the distinction between these two kinds of distance assumes special importance theoretically in the differentiation between sculpture in the round, and relief-sculpture. Temporal distance, remoteness from us in point of time, though often a cause of misconceptions, has been declared to be a factor of considerable weight in our appreciation.

It is not, however, in any of these meanings that

57

'Distance' is put forward here, though it will be clear
in the course of this essay that the above mentioned kinds
of distance are rather special forms of the conception of
Distance as advocated here, and derive whatever aesthetic
qualities they may possess from Distance in its general
connotation. This general connotation is 'Psychical
Distance.'

A short illustration will explain what is meant by
'Psychical Distance.' Imagine a fog at sea: for most
people it is an experience of acute unpleasantness.
Apart from the physical annoyance and remoter forms of
discomfort such as delays, it is apt to produce feelings
of peculiar anxiety, fears of invisible dangers, strains of
watching and listening for distant and unlocalised signals.
The listless movements of the ship and her warning calls
soon tell upon the nerves of the passengers; and that special,
expectant, tacit anxiety and nervousness, always associated
with this experience, make a fog the dreaded terror of the
sea (all the more terrifying because of its very silence and
gentleness) for the expert seafarer no less than for the
ignorant landsman.

58

Nevertheless, a fog at sea can be a source of intense relish and enjoyment. Abstract from the experience of the sea fog, for the moment, its danger and practical unpleasantness, just as every one in the enjoyment of a mountain - climb disregards its physical labour and its danger (though, it is not denied, that these may incidentally enter into the enjoyment and enhance it); direct the attention to the features 'objectively' constituting the phenomenon - the veil surrounding you with an opaqueness as of transparent milk, blurring the outline of things and distorting their shapes into weird grotesqueness; observe the carrying-power of the air, producing the impression as if you could touch some far-off siren by merely putting out your hand and letting it lose itself behind that white wall; note the curious creamy smoothness of the water, hypocritically denying as it were any suggestion of danger; and, above all, the strange solitude and remoteness from the world, as it can be found only on the highest mountain tops: and the experience may acquire, in its uncanny mingling of repose and terror, a flavour of such concentrated poignancy and delight as to contrast sharply with the blind and distempered anxiety

59

of its other aspects. This contrast, often emerging with startling suddenness, is like a momentary switching on of some new current, or the passing ray of a brighter light, illuminating the outlook upon perhaps the most ordinary and familiar objects - an impression which we experience sometimes in instants of direst extremity, when our practical interest snaps like a wire from sheer over-tension, and we watch the consummation of some impending catastrophe with the marvelling unconcern of a mere spectator.

It is a difference of outlook, due - if such a metaphor is permissible - to the insertion of Distance. This Distance appears to lie between our own self and its affections, using the latter term in its broadest sense as anything which affects our being, bodily or spiritually, e.g. as sensation, perception, emotional state or idea. Usually, though not always, it amounts to the same thing to say that the Distance lies between our own self and such objects as are the sources or vehicles of such affections.

Thus, in the fog, the transformation by Distance is produced in the first instance by putting the phenomenon, so to speak, out of gear with our practical, actual self; by allowing it to stand outside the context of our personal needs and ends - in short, by looking at it 'objectively', as it has often been called, by permitting only such reactions on our part as emphasise the 'objective' features of the experience, and by interpreting even our 'subjective' affections not as modes of our being but rather as characteristics of the phenomenon.

The working of Distance is, accordingly, not simple, but highly complex. It has a negative, inhibitory aspect - the cutting-out of the practical sides of things and of our practical attitude to them - and a positive side - the elaboration of the experience on the new basis created by the inhibitory action of Distance.

2. Consequently, this distanced view of things is not, and cannot be, our normal outlook. As a rule, experiences constantly turn the same side towards us, namely, that which has the strongest practical force of appeal. We are not ordinarily aware of those aspects of things which do not touch us immediately and practically, nor are we generally conscious of impressions apart from our own self which is

impressed. The sudden view of things from their reverse, usually unnoticed, side, comes upon us as a revelation, and such revelations are precisely those of Art. In this most general sense, Distance is a factor in all Art.

3. It is, for this very reason, also an aesthetic principle. The aesthetic contemplation and the aesthetic outlook have often been described as 'objective.' We speak of 'objective' artists as Shakespeare or Velasquez, of 'objective' works or art forms, as Homer's Iliad or the drama. It is a term constantly occurring in discussions and criticisms, though its sense if pressed at all, becomes very questionable. For certain forms of Art, such as lyrical poetry, are said to be 'subjective' ..... On the other hand, no work of Art can be genuinely 'objective' in the sense in which this term might be applied to a work on history or to a scientific treatise; nor can it be 'subjective' in the ordinary acceptance of that term, as a personal feeling, a direct statement of a wish or belief, or a cry of passion is subjective. 'Objectivity' and 'subjectivity' are a pair of opposites which in their mutual exclusiveness when applied to Art soon lead to confusion

Nor are they the only pair of opposites. Art has with

equal vigour been declared alternately 'idealistic' and 'realistic,' 'sensual' and 'spiritual,' 'individualistic' and 'typical.' Between the defence of either terms of such antitheses most aesthetic theories have vacillated. It is one of the contentions of this essay that such opposites find their synthesis in the more fundamental conception of Distance.

Distance further provides the much needed criterion of the beautiful as distinct from the merely agreeable.

Again, it marks one of the most important steps in the process of artistic creation and serves as a distinguishing feature of what is commonly so loosely described as the 'artistic temperament.'

Finally, it may claim to be considered as one of the essential characteristics of the 'aesthetic consciousness,' - if I may describe by this term that special mental attitude towards, and outlook upon, experience, which finds its most pregnant expression in the various forms of Art.

II.

Distance, as I said before, is obtained by separating the object and its appeal from one's own self, by putting it out of gear with practical needs and ends. Thereby the 'contemplation' of the object becomes alone possible. But it does not mean that the relation between the self and the object is broken to the extent of becoming 'impersonal.' Of the alternatives 'personal' and 'impersonal' the latter surely comes nearer to the truth; but here, as elsewhere, we meet the difficulty of having to express certain facts in terms coined for entirely different uses. To do so usually results in paradoxes, which are nowhere more inevitable than in discussions upon Art. 'Personal' and 'impersonal,' 'subjective' and 'objective' are such terms, devised for purposes other than aesthetic speculation, and becoming loose and ambiguous as soon as applied outside the sphere of their special meanings. In giving preference therefore to the term 'impersonal' to describe the relation between the spectator and a work of Art, it is to be noticed that it is not impersonal in the sense in which we speak of the 'impersonal' character of Science, for instance. In order to obtain 'objectively valid' results, the scientist excludes the 'personal factor,' i.e. his personal wishes as to the validity of his results, his predilection for any

particular system to be proved or disproved by his research.
It goes without saying that all experiments and investigations
are undertaken out of a personal interest in the science,
for the ultimate support of a definite assumption, and involve
personal hopes of success; but this does not affect the
'dispassionate' attitude of the investigator, under pain
of being accused of 'manufacturing his evidence.'

1. Distance does not imply an impersonal, purely
intellectually interested relation of such a kind. On the
contrary, it describes a _personal_ relation, often highly
emotionally coloured, but_of a peculiar character._ Its
peculiarity lies in that the personal character of the
relation has been, so to speak, filtered. It has been
cleared of the practical, concrete nature of its appeal,
without, however, thereby losing its original constitution.
One of the best-known examples is to be found in our attitude
towards the events and characters of the drama: they appeal
to us like persons and incidents of normal experience,
except that that side of their appeal, which would usually
affect us in a directly personal manner, is held in abeyance.
This difference, so well known as to be almost trivial, is

generally explained by reference to the knowledge that the characters and situations are 'unreal', imaginary. In this sense Witasek,[1] operating with Meinong's theory of _Annahmen_, has described the emotions involved in witnessing a drama as _Scheingefuhle_, a term which has so frequently been misunderstood in discussions of his theories. But, as a matter of fact, the 'assumption' upon which the imaginative emotional reaction is based is not necessarily the condition, but often the consequence, of Distance; that is to say, the converse of the reason usually stated would then be true: viz, that Distance, by changing our relation to the characters, renders them seemingly fictitious . . . . . It is, of course, to be granted that the actual and admitted unreality of the dramatic action reinforces the effect of Distance. But surely the proverbial unsophisticated yokel whose chivalrous interference in the play on behalf of the hapless heroine can only be prevented by impressing upon him that 'they are only pretending,' is not the ideal type of theatrical

---

1 H. Witasek, 'Zur psychologischen Analyse der aesthetischen Einfuhlung,' _Ztsch. f. Psychol. u. Physiol. der Sinnesorg._ 1901, XXV. 1 ff.; _Grundzilge der Aesthetik_, Leipzig, 1904.

audience. The proof of the seeming paradox that it is
Distance which primarily gives to dramatic action the appearance
of unreality and not _vice versa_, is the observation that the
same filtration of our sentiments and the same seeming
'unreality' of _actual_ men and things occur, when at times,
by a sudden change of inward perspective, we are overcome
by the feeling that 'all the world's a stage.'

2. This personal, but 'distanced' relation (as I will
venture to call this nameless character of our view) directs
attention to a strange fact which appears to be one of the
fundamental paradoxes of Art: it is what I propose to call
'the antinomy of Distance.'

It will be readily admitted that a work of Art has the
more chance of appealing to us the better it finds us prepared
for its particular kind of appeal. Indeed, without some degree
of predisposition on our part, it must necessarily remain
incomprehensible, and to that extent unappreciated. The
success and intensity of its appeal would seem, therefore,
to stand in direct proportion to the completeness with
which it corresponds with our intellectual and emotional
peculiarities and the idiosyncracies of our experience. The

absence of such a concordance between the characters of
a work and of the spectator is, of course, the most general
explanation for differences of 'tastes.'

At the same time, such a principle of concordance
requires a qualification, which leads at once to the antinomy
of Distance.

Suppose a man, who believes that he has cause to be
jealous about his wife, witnesses a performance of 'Othello.'
He will the more perfectly appreciate the situation, conduct
and character of Othello, the more exactly the feelings and
experiences of Othello coincide with his own - at least he
ought to on the above principle of concordance. In point
of fact, he will probably do anything but appreciate the
play. In reality, the concordance will merely render him
acutely conscious of his own jealousy; by a sudden reversal
of perspective he will no longer see Othello apparently
betrayed by Desdemona, but himself in an analogous situation
with his own wife. This reversal of perspective is the
consequence of the loss of Distance.

If this be taken as a typical case, it follows that the
qualification required is that the coincidence should be as

complete as is compatible with maintaining Distance.
The jealous spectator of 'Othello' will indeed appreciate
and enter into the play the more keenly, the greater
the resemblance with his own experience - provided that
he succeeds in keeping the Distance between the action of
the play and his personal feelings: a very difficult performance in the circumstances. It is on account of the
same difficulty that the expert and the professional critic
make a bad audience, since their expertness and critical pro-
fessionalism are practical activities, involving their concrete
personality and constantly endangering their Distance. It is,
by the way, one of the reasons why Criticism is an art, for it
requires the constant interchange from the practical to the
distanced attitude and vice versa, which is characteristic of
artists.

The same qualification applies to the artist. He will
prove artistically most effective in the formulation of an
intensely personal experience, but he can formulate it
artistically only on condition of a detachment from the
experience . . . . qua personal.
Hence the statement of so many artists that artistic

formulations was to them a kind of catharsis, a means of
ridding themselves of feelings and ideas the acuteness
of which they felt almost as a kind of obsession. Hence,
on the other hand, the failure of the average man to convey
to others at all adequately the impression of an over-
whelming joy or sorrow. His personal implication in the
event renders it impossible for him to formulate and
present it in such a way as to make others, like himself,
feel all the meaning and fulness which it possesses for
him.

What is therefore, both in appreciation and production,
most desirable is the <u>utmost decrease of Distance without
its disappearance.</u>

3. Closely related, in fact a presupposition to the
'antinomy,' is the <u>variability of Distance.</u> Herein especially
lies the advantage of Distance compared with such terms as
'objectivity' and 'detachment.' Neither of them implies
a personal relation - indeed both actually preclude it;
and the mere inflexibility and exclusiveness of their
opposites render their application generally meaningless.

Distance, on the contrary, admits naturally of degrees,

70

and differs not only according to the nature of the object, which may impose a greater or smaller degree of Distance, but varies also according to the individual's capacity for maintaining a greater or lesser degree. And here one may remark that not only do persons differ from each other in their habitual measure of Distance, but that the same individual differs in his ability to maintain it in the face of different objects and of different arts.

There exist, therefore, two different sets of conditions affecting the degree of Distance in any given case: those offered by the object and those realised by the subject. In their interplay they afford one of the most extensive explanations for varieties of aesthetic experience, since loss of Distance, whether due to the one or the other, means loss of aesthetic appreciation.

In short, Distance may be said to be variable both according to the distancing-power of the individual, and according to the character of the object.

There are two ways of losing Distance: either to 'under-distance' or to 'over-distance.' 'Under-distancing' is the commonest failing of the subject, an excess of

Distance is a frequent failing of <u>Art,</u> especially in the past. Historically it looks almost as if Art had attempted to meet the deficiency of Distance on the part of the subject and had overshot the mark in this endeavour. It will be seen later that this is actually true, for it appears that over-distanced Art is specially designed for a class of appreciation which has difficulty to rise spontaneously to any degree of Distance. The consequence of a loss of Distance through one or other cause is familiar: the verdict in the case of under-distancing is that the work is 'crudely naturalistic,' 'harrowing,' 'repulsive in its realism.' An excess of distance produces the impression of improbability, artificiality, emptiness or absurdity.

The individual tends, as I just stated, to under-distance rather than to lose Distance by over-distancing. <u>Theoretically</u> there is no limit to the decrease of Distance. In theory, therefore, not only the usual subjects of Art, but even the most personal affections, whether ideas, percepts or emotions, can be sufficiently distanced to be aesthetically appreciable. Especially artists are gifted in this direction to a remark-able extent. The average individual, on the contrary, very

72

rapidly reaches his limit of decreasing Distance, his 'Distance-limit,' i.e. that point at which Distance is lost and appreciation either disappears or changes its character. In the practice, therefore, of the average person, a limit does exist which marks the minimum at which his appreciation can maintain itself in the aesthetic field, and this average minimum lies considerably higher than the Distance-limit of the artist. It is practically impossible to fix this average limit, in the absence of data, and on account of the wide fluctuations from person to person to which this limit is subject. But it is safe to infer that, in art practice, explicit references to organic affections, to the material existence of the body, especially to sexual matters, lie normally below the Distance-limit, and can be touched upon by Art only with special precautions. Allusions to social institutions of any degree of personal importance - in particular, allusions implying any doubt as to their validity - the questioning of some generally recognised ethical sanctions, references to topical subjects occupying public attention at the moment, and such like, are all dangerously near the average limit

73

and may at any time fall below it, arousing, instead of
aesthetic appreciation, concrete hostility or mere amusement.

This difference in the Distance-limit between artists
and the public has been the source of much misunderstanding
and injustice. Many an artist has seen his work condemned,
and himself ostracized for the sake of so-called 'immoralities'
which to him were <u>bona fide</u> aesthetic objects. His power of
distancing, nay, the necessity of distancing feelings,
sensations, situations, which for the average person are too
intimately bound up with his concrete existence to be regarded
in that light, have often quite unjustly earned for him
accusations of cynicism, sensualism, morbidness or frivolity.
The same misconception has arisen over many 'problem plays'
and 'problem novels' in which the public have persisted in
seeing nothing but a supposed 'problem' of the moment,
whereas the author may have been - and often has demonstrably
been - able to distance the subject-matter sufficiently to
rise above its practical problematic import and to regard
it simply as a dramatically and humanly interesting situation.

The variability of Distance in respect to Art, dis-
regarding for the moment the subjective complication, appears

74

both as a general feature in Art, and in the differences between the special arts.

It has been an old problem why the 'arts of the eye and of the ear' should have reached the practically exclusive predominance over arts of other senses. Attempts to raise 'culinary art' to the level of a Fine Art have failed in spite of all propaganda, as completely as the creation of scent or liqueur 'symphonies.' There is little doubt that, apart from other excellent reasons [1] of a partly psycho-physical, partly technical nature, the actual, <u>spatial distance</u> separating objects of sight and hearing from the subject has contributed strongly to the development of this monopoly. In a similar manner <u>temporal remoteness</u> produces Distance, and objects removed from us in point of time are <u>ipso facto</u> distanced to an extent which was impossible for their contemporaries. Many pictures, plays and poems had, as a matter of fact, rather an expository or illustrative significance - as for instance much ecclesiastical

---

1 J. Volkelt, 'Die Bedeutung der niederen Empfindungen fur die aesthetische Einfuhlung,' <u>Ztsch. fur Psychol. u. Physiol. der Sinnesorg.</u> XXXII. 15, 16; <u>System der Aesthetik</u>, 1905, I.260

Art - or the force of a direct practical appeal - as the invectives of many satires or comedies - which seem to us nowadays irreconcilable with their aesthetic claims. Such works have consequently profited greatly by lapse of time and have reached the level of Art only with the help of temporal distance, while others, on the contrary, often for the same reason have suffered a loss of Distance, through over-distancing.

Special mention must be made of a group of artistic conceptions which present excessive Distance in their form of appeal rather than in their actual presentation - a point illustrating the necessity of distinguishing between distancing an object and distancing the appeal of which it is the source. I mean here what is often rather loosely termed 'idealistic Art,' that is, Art springing from abstract conceptions, expressing allegorical meanings, or illustrating general truths. Generalisations and abstractions suffer under this disadvantage that they have too much general applicability to invite a personal interest in them, and too little individual concreteness to prevent them applying to us in all their force. They appeal to everybody and

76

and therefore to none. An axiom of Euclid belongs to nobody, just because it compels everyone's assent; general conceptions like Patriotism, Friendship, Love, Hope, Life, Death, concern as much Dick, Tom and Harry as myself, and I, therefore, either feel unable to get into any kind of personal relation to them, or, if I do so, they become at once, emphatically and concretely, my Patriotism, my Friendship, my Love, my Hope, my Life and Death. By mere force of generalisation, a general truth or a universal ideal is so far distanced from myself that I fail to realise it concretely at all, or, when I do so, I can realise it only as part of my practical actual being, i.e. it falls below the Distance-limit altogether. 'Idealistic Art' suffers consequently under the peculiar difficulty that its excess of Distance turns generally into an under-distanced appeal - all the more easily, as it is the usual failing of the subject to under - rather than to over-distance.

The different special arts show at the present time very marked variations in the degree of Distance which they usually impose or require for their appreciation. Unfortunately here again the absence of data makes itself felt and indicates the necessity of conducting observations, possibly experiments, so as to place these suggestions upon a securer basis. In one single art, viz. the theatre, a small amount of information is available, from an unexpected source, namely the proceedings of the censorship committee, [1] which on closer examination might be made to yield evidence of interest to the psychologist. In fact, the whole censorship problem, as far as it does not turn upon purely economic questions, may be said to hinge upon Distance. If every member of the public could be trusted to keep it, there would be no sense whatever in the existence of a censor of plays. There is, of course, no doubt that, speaking generally, theatrical performances eo ipso run a special risk of a loss of Distance owing to the material presentment [2] of its subject-matter. The physical presence of living human beings as vehicles of dramatic art is a difficulty which no art has to face in the same way. A

---

1 Report from the Joint Select Committee of the House of Lords and the House of Commons on the Stage Plays (Censorship), 1909.
2 I shall use the term 'presentment' to denote the manner of presenting, in distinction to 'presentation' as that which is presented.

similar, in many ways even greater, risk confronts dancing: though attracting perhaps a less widely spread human interest, its animal spirits are frequently quite unrelieved by any glimmer of spirituality and consequently form a proportionately stronger lure to under-distancing. In the higher forms of dancing technical execution of the most wearing kind makes up a great deal for its intrinsic tendency towards a loss of Distance, and as a popular performance, at least in southern Europe, it has retained much of its ancient artistic glamour, producing a peculiarly subtle balancing of Distance between the pure delight of bodily movement and high technical accomplishment. In passing, it is interesting to observe (as bearing upon the development of Distance), that this art, once as much a fine art as music and considered by the Greeks as a particularly valuable educational exercise, should - except in sporadic cases - have fallen so low from the pedestal it once occupied. Next to the theatre and dancing stands sculpture. Though not using a living bodily medium, yet the human form in its full spatial materiality constitutes a similar threat to Distance. Our northern habits of dress and ignorance of the human body have

79

enormously increased the difficulty of distancing Sculpture,
in part through the gross misconceptions to which it is
exposed, in part owing to a complete lack of standards of
bodily perfection, and an inability to realise the distinction
between sculptural form and bodily shape, which is the only
but fundamental point distinguishing a statue from a cast
taken from life. In painting it is apparently the form of
its presentment and the usual reduction in scale which
would explain why this art can venture to approach more
closely than sculpture to the normal Distance-limit. As
this matter will be discussed later in a special connexion
this simple reference may suffice here. Music and architecture have a curious position. These two most abstract
of all arts show a remarkable fluctuation in their Distances.
Certain kinds of music, especially 'pure' music, or'classical'
or 'heavy' music, appear for many people over-distanced;
light, 'catchy' tunes, on the contrary, easily reach that
degree of decreasing Distance below which they cease to be
Art and become a pure amusement. In spite of its strange
abstractness which to many philosophers has made it comparable
to architecture and mathematics, music possesses a sensuous,

80

frequently sensual, character: the undoubted physiological
and muscular stimulus of its melodies and harmonies, no less
than its rhythmic aspects, would seem to account for the
occasional disappearance of Distance. To this might be
added its strong tendency, especially in unmusical people,
to stimulate trains of thought quite disconnected with
itself, following channels of subjective inclinations, -
day-dreams of a more or less directly personal character.
Architecture requires almost uniformly a very great Distance;
that is to say, the majority of persons derive no aesthetic
appreciation from architecture as such, apart from the
incidental impression of its decorative features and its
associations. The causes are numerous, but prominent
among them are the confusion of building with architecture
and the predominance of utilitarian purposes, which over-
shadow the architectural claims upon the attention.

4. That all art requires a Distance-limit beyond which,
and a Distance within which only, aesthetic appreciation becomes
possible, is the psychological formulation of a general
characteristic of Art, viz. its anti-realistic nature. Though
seemingly paradoxical, this applies as much to 'naturalistic'

as to 'idealistic' Art. The difference commonly expressed by these epithets is at bottom merely the difference in the degree of Distance; and this produces, so far as 'naturalism' and 'idealism' in Art are not meaningless labels, the usual result that what appears obnoxiously 'naturalistic' to one person, may be 'idealistic' to another. To say that Art is anti-realistic simply insists upon the fact that Art is not nature, never pretends to be nature and strongly resists any confusion with nature. It emphasizes the art-character of Art: 'artistic' is synonymous with 'anti-realistic'; it explains even sometimes a very marked degree of artificiality.

'Art is an imitation of nature,' was the current art-conception in the 18th century. It is the fundamental axiom of the standard-work of that time upon aesthetic theory by the Abbe Du Bos, Reflexions critiques sur la poesie et la peinture, 1719; the idea received strong support from the literal acceptance of Aristotle's theory of mimesis and produced echoes everywhere, in Lessing's Laocoon no less than in Burke's famous statement that 'all Art is great as it deceives.' Though it may be assumed that since the time

82

of Kant and of the Romanticists this notion has died out, it still lives in unsophisticated minds. Even when formally denied, it persists, for instance, in the belief that 'Art idealises nature,' which means after all only that Art copies nature with certain improvements and revisions. Artists themselves are unfortunately often responsible for the spreading of this conception. Whistler indeed said that to produce Art by imitating nature would be like trying to produce music by sitting upon the piano, but the selective, idealising imitation of nature finds merely another support in such a saying. Naturalism, pleinairism, impressionism, - even the guileless enthusiasm of the artist for the works of nature, her wealth of suggestion, her delicacy of work-manship, for the steadfastness of her guidance, only produce upon the public the impression that Art is, after all, an imitation of nature. Then how can it be anti-realistic? The antithesis, Art _versus_ nature, seems to break down. Yet if it does, what is the sense of Art?

Here the conception of Distance comes to the rescue. The solution of the dilemma lies in the 'antinomy of Distance' with its demand: utmost decrease of Distance without its disappearance.

The simple observation that Art is the more effective, the
more it falls into line with our predispositions which are
inevitably moulded on general experience and nature, has
always been the original motive for 'naturalism.'
'Naturalism,' 'impressionism' is no new thing; it is only
a new name for an innate leaning of Art, from the time of
the Chaldeans and Egyptians down to the present day. Even
the Apollo of Tenea apparently struck his contemporaries
as so startlingly 'naturalistic' that the subsequent
legend attributed a superhuman genius to his creator. A
constantly closer approach to nature, a perpetual refining
of the limit of Distance, yet without overstepping the
dividing line of art and nature, has always been the
inborn bent of art. To deny this dividing line has
occasionally been the failing of naturalism. But no
theory of naturalism is complete which does not at the
same time allow for the intrinsic idealism of Art: for
both are merely degrees in that wide range lying beyond
the Distance-limit. To imitate nature so as to trick the
spectator into the deception that it is nature which he
beholds, is to forsake Art, its anti-realism, its distanced

84

spirituality, and to fall below the limit into sham, sensationalism or platitude.

But what, in the theory of antinomy of Distance requires explanation is the existence of an _idealistic, highly distanced_ Art. There are numerous reasons to account for it; indeed in so complex a phenomenon as Art, _single_ causes can be pronounced almost _a priori_ to be false. Foremost among such causes which have contributed to the formation of an idealistic Art appears to stand the subordination of Art to some extraneous purpose of an impressive, exceptional character. Such a subordination has consisted - at various epochs of Art history - in the use to which Art was put to subserve commemorative, hieratic, generally religious, royal or patriotic functions. The object to be commemorated had to stand out from among other still existing objects or persons; the thing or the being to be worshipped had to be distinguished as markedly as possible from profaner objects of reverence and had to be invested with an air of sanctity by a removal from its ordinary context of occurrence. Nothing could have assisted more powerfully the introduction of a high Distance than this attempt

to differentiate objects of common experience in order to fit
them for their exalted position. Curious, unusual things of
nature met this tendency half-way and easily assumed divine
rank; but others had to be distanced by an exaggeration of
their size, by extraordinary attributes, by strange combinations of human and animal forms, by special insistence
upon particular characteristics, or by the careful removal
of all noticeably individualistic and concrete features.
Nothing could be more striking than the contrast, for example,
in Egyptian Art between the monumental, stereotyped effigies
of the Pharaohs, and the startlingly realistic rendering of
domestic scenes and of ordinary mortals, such as 'the Scribe'
or 'the Village Sehikh.' Equally noteworthy is the exceeding
artificiality of Russian eikon-painting with its prescribed
attributes, expressions and gestures. Even Greek dramatic
practice appears to have aimed, for similar purposes and in
marked contrast to our stage-habits, at an increase rather
than at a decrease of Distance. Otherwise Greek Art, even
of a religious type, is remarkable for its <u>low</u> Distance
value; and it speaks highly for the aesthetic capacities
of the Greeks that the degree of realism which they ventured

86

to impart to the representations of their gods, while
humanising them did not, at least at first [1], impair the
reverence of their feelings towards them. But apart from
such special causes, idealistic Art of great Distance has
appeared at intervals, for apparently no other reason than
that the great Distance was felt to be essential to its
art-character. What is noteworthy and runs counter to
many accepted ideas is that such periods were usually epochs
of a low level of general culture. These were times, which,
like childhood, required the marvellous, the extraordinary,
to satisfy their artistic longings, and neither realised
nor cared for the poetic or artistic qualities of ordinary
things. They were frequently times, in which the mass of
the people were plunged in ignorance and buried under a
load of misery, and in which even the small educated class
sought rather amusement or a pastime in Art; or they were
epochs of a strong practical common-sense too much concerned

---

1 That this practice did, in course of time, undermine their
  religious faith, is clear from the plays of Euripides and
  from Plato's condemnation of Homer's mythology.

with the rough-and-tumble of life to have any sense of its
aesthetic charms.   Art was to them what melodrama is to
a section of the public at the present time, and its wide
Distance was the safeguard of its artistic character.   The
flowering periods of Art have, on the contrary, always
borne the evidence of a narrow Distance.   Greek Art, as
just mentioned, was realistic to an extent which we,
spoilt as we are by modern developments, can grasp with
difficulty, but which the contrast with its oriental
contemporaries sufficiently proves.   During the Augustan
period - which Art historians at last are coming to regard
no longer as merely 'degenerated' Greek Art - Roman Art
achieved its greatest triumphs in an almost naturalistic
portrait-sculpture.   In the Renaissance we need only think
of the realism of portraiture, sometimes amounting almost
to cynicism, of the desinvolture with which the mistresses
of popes and dukes were posed as madonnas, saints and goddesses
apparently without any detriment to the aesthetic appeal
of the works, and of the remarkable interpenetration of
Art with the most ordinary routine of life, in order to
realise the scarcely perceptible dividing line between

88

the sphere of Art and the realm of practical existence. In a sense, the assertion that idealistic Art marks periods of a generally low and narrowly restricted culture is the converse to the oft-repeated statement that the flowering periods of Art coincide with epochs of decadence: for this so-called decadence represents indeed in certain respects a process of disintegration, politically, racially, often nationally, but a disruption necessary to the formation of larger social units and to the breakdown of out-grown national restrictions. For this very reason it has usually also been the sign of the growth of personal independence and of an expansion of individual culture.

To proceed to some more special points illustrating the distanced and therefore anti-realistic character of art, - both in subject-matter and in the form of presentation Art has always safeguarded its distanced view. Fanciful, even phantastic, subjects have from time immemorial been the accredited material of Art. No doubt things, as well as our view of them, have changed in the course of time: Polyphemus and the Lotus-Eaters for the Greeks, the Venusberg or the Magnetic Mountain for the Middle Ages were less incredible,

more realistic than to us. But Peter Pan or L'Oiseau Bleu
still appeal at the present day in spite of the prevailing
note of realism of our time. 'Probability' and 'improbability'
in Art are not to be measured by their correspondence (or
lack of it) with actual experience. To do so had involved
the theories of the 15th to the 18th centuries in endless
contradictions. It is rather a matter of consistency of
Distance. The note of realism, set by a work as a whole,
determines intrinsically the greater or smaller degree of
fancy which it permits; and consequently we feel the loss of
Peter Pan's shadow to be infinitely more probable than some
trifling improbability which shocks our sense of proportion
in a naturalistic work. No doubt also, fairy-tales, fairy-
plays, stories of strange adventures were primarily
invented to satisfy the craving of curiosity, the desire
for the marvellous, the shudder of the unwonted and the
longing for imaginary experiences. But by their mere
eccentricity in regard to the normal facts of experience
they cannot have failed to arouse a strong feeling of
Distance.

Again, certain conventional subjects taken from

90

mythical and legendary traditions, at first closely connected
with the concrete, practical, life of a devout public, have
gradually, by the mere force of convention as much as by
their inherent anti-realism, acquired Distance for us today.
Our view of Greek mythological sculpture, of early Christian
saints and martyrs must be considerably distanced, compared
with that of the Greek and medieval worshipper. It is in
part the result of lapse of time, but in part also a real
change of attitude. Already the outlook of the Imperial
Roman had altered, and Pausanias shows a curious dualism
of standpoint, declaring the Athene Lemnia to be the
supreme achievement of Phidias's genius, and gazing awe-
struck upon the roughly hewn tree-trunk representing some
primitive Apollo. Our understanding of Greek tragedy
suffers admittedly under our inability to revert to the
point of view for which it was originally written. Even
the tragedies of Racine demand an imaginative effort to
put ourselves back into the courtly atmosphere of red-heeled,
powdered ceremony. Provided the Distance is not too wide,
the result of its intervention has everywhere been to enhance
the art-character of such works and to lower their original

91

ethical and social force of appeal. Thus in the central dome of the Church (Sta Maria dei Miracoli) at Saronno are depicted the heavenly hosts in ascending tiers, crowned by the benevolent figure of the Divine Father, bending from the window of heaven to bestow His blessing upon the assembled community. The mere realism of foreshortening and of the boldest vertical perspective may well have made the naive Christian of the 16th century conscious of the Divine Presence - but for us it has become a work of Art.

The unusual, exceptional, has found its especial home in tragedy. It has always - except in highly distanced tragedy - been a popular objection to it that 'there is enough sadness in life without going to the theatre for it.' Already Aristotle appears to have met with this view among his contemporaries clamouring for 'happy endings.' Yet tragedy is not sad; if it were, there would indeed be little sense in its existence. For the tragic is just in so far different from the merely sad, as it is distanced; and it is largely the exceptional which produces the Distance of tragedy: exceptional situations, exceptional characters, exceptional destinies and conduct. Not of course, characters

92

merely cranky, eccentric, pathological. The exceptional
element in tragic figures - that which makes them so
utterly different from characters we meet with in ordinary
experience - is a consistency of direction, a fervour of
ideality, a persistence and driving-force which is far above
the capacities of average men. The tragic of tragedy
would, transposed into ordinary life, in nine cases out of
ten, end in drama, in comedy, even in farce, for lack
of steadfastness, for fear of conventions, for the dread
of 'scenes,' for a hundred-and-one petty faithlessnesses
towards a belief or an ideal: even if for none of these,
it would end in a compromise simply because man forgets
and time heals.[1] Again, the sympathy, which aches with

---

1 The famous 'unity of time,' so senseless as a 'canon,' is
all the same often an indispensable condition of tragedy.
For in many a tragedy the catastrophe would be even intrinsically
impossible, if fatality did not overtake the hero with that
rush which gives no time to forget and none to heal. It is
in cases such as these that criticism has often blamed the
work for 'improbability' - the old confusion between Art and
nature - forgetting that the death of the hero is the convention of the art-form, as much as grouping in a picture
is such a convention and that probability is not the
correspondence with average experience, but consistency of
Distance.

the sadness of tragedy is another such confusion, the under-distancing of tragedy's appeal. Tragedy trembles always on the knife-edge of a _personal_ reaction, and sympathy which finds relief in tears tends almost always towards a loss of Distance. Such a loss naturally renders tragedy unpleasant to a degree: it becomes sad, dismal, harrowing, depressing. But real tragedy (melodrama has a very strong tendency to speculate upon sympathy), truly appreciated, is not sad. 'The pity of it - oh, the pity of it,' that essence of all genuine tragedy is not the pity of mild, regretful sympathy. It is a chaos of tearless, bitter bewilderment, of upsurging revolt and rapturous awe before the ruthless and inscrutable fate; it is the homage to the great and exceptional in the man who in a last effort of spiritual tension can rise to confront blind, crowning Necessity even in his crushing defeat.

As I explained earlier, the form of presentation some-times endangers the maintenance of Distance, but it more frequently acts as a considerable support. Thus the bodily vehicle of _drama_ is the chief factor of risk to Distance. But, as if to counterbalance a confusion with nature, other

94

features of stage-presentation exercise an opposite influence.
Such are the general theatrical milieu, the shape and arrangement of the stage, the artificial lighting, the costumes,
mise-en-scene and make-up, even the language, especially verse.
Modern reforms of staging, aiming primarily at the removal
of artistic incongruities between excessive decoration and
and the living figures of the actors and at the production
of a more homogeneous stage-picture, inevitably work also
towards a greater emphasis and homogeneity of Distance.
The history of staging and dramaturgy is closely bound up
with the evolution of Distance, and its fluctuations lie
at the bottom not only of the greater part of all the talk
and writing about 'dramatic probability' and the Aristotelian
'unities,' but also of 'theatrical illusion.' In sculpture,
one distancing factor of presentment is its lack of colour.
The aesthetic, or rather inaesthetic effect of realistic
colouring, is in no way touched by the controversial question
of its use historically; its attempted resuscitation, such
as by Klinger, seems only to confirm its disadvantages. The
distancing use even of pedestals, although originally no
doubt serving other purposes, is evident to anyone who has

95

experienced the oppressively crowded sensation of moving
in a room among life-sized statues placed directly upon the
floor. The circumstance that the space of statuary is the
same space as ours (in distinction to relief sculpture or
painting, for instance) renders a distancing by pedestals,
i.e. a removal from our spatial context, imperative.[1]
Probably the framing of <u>pictures</u> might be shown to serve
a similar purpose - though paintings have intrinsically
ạ much greater Dịstancẹ - becausẹ neiLhẹi Lhẹiг ѕpạ¢ẹ
(perspective an imaginary space) nor their lighting
coincides with our (actual) space or light, and the usual
reduction in scale of the represented objects prevents a
feeling of undue proximity. Besides, painting always
retains to some extent a <u>two</u>-dimensional character, and
this character supplies <u>eo ipso</u> a Distance. Nevertheless,
life-size pictures, especially if they possess strong relief,
and their light happens to coincide with the actual lighting,

---

1 An instance which might be adduced to disprove this point
  only shows its correctness on closer inspection: for it
  was on purpose and with the intention of removing Distance,
  that Rodin originally intended his <u>citoyens de Calais</u> to be
  placed, without pedestals, upon the market-place of that town.

can occasionally produce the impression of actual presence which is a far from pleasant, though fortunately only a passing, illusion. For decorative purposes, in pictorial renderings of vistas, garden-perspectives and architectural extensions, the removal of Distance has often been consciously striven after, whether with aesthetically satisfactory results is much disputed.

A general help towards Distance (and therewith an anti-realistic feature) is to be found in the 'unification of presentment[2]' of all art-objects. By unification of presentment are meant such qualities as symmetry, opposition, proportion, balance, rhythmical distribution of parts, light-arrangements, in fact all so-called 'formal' features, 'composition' in the widest sense. Unquestionably, Distance is not the only, nor even the principal function of composition; it serves to render our grasp of the presentation easier and to increase its intelligibility. It may even in itself constitute the principal aesthetic feature of the object, as in linear complexes or patterns, partly also in architectural

---

2 See note 2, p. 78.

designs. Yet, its distancing effect can hardly be underrated.

For, every kind of visibly intentional arrangement or unificatic

must, by the mere fact of its presence, enforce Distance, by

distinguishing the object from the confused, disjointed and

scattered forms of actual experience. This function can be

gauged in a typical form in cases where composition produces

an exceptionally marked impression of artificiality (not in

the bad sense of that term, but in the sense in which all art

is artificial); and it is a natural corollary to the differences

of Distance in different arts and of different subjects, that

the arts and subjects vary in the degree of artificiality which

they bear. It is this sense of artificial finish which is

the source of so much of that elaborate charm of Byzantine

work, of Mohammedan decoration, of the hieratic stiffness

of so many primitive madonnas and saints. In general the

emphasis of composition and technical finish increases with

the Distance of the subject-matter: heroic conceptions lend

themselves better to verse than to prose; monumental statues

require a more general treatment, more elaboration of setting

and artificiality of pose than impressionistic statuettes

like those of Troubetzkoi; an ecclesiastic subject is painted

98

with a degree of symmetrical arrangement which would be ridiculous in a Dutch interior, and a naturalistic drama carefully avoids the tableau impression characteristic of a mystery play. In a similar manner the variations of Distance in the arts go hand in hand with a visibly greater predominance of composition and 'formal' elements, reaching a climax in architecture and music. It is again a matter of 'consistency of Distance.' At the same time . . . from the point of view of the public the emphasis of composition and technical finish appears frequently to relieve the impression of highly distanced subjects by diminishing the Distance of the whole. The spectator has a tendency to see in composition and finish merely evidence of the artist's 'cleverness,' of his mastery over his material. Manual dexterity is an enviable thing to possess in everyone's experience, and naturally appeals to the public practically, thereby putting it into a directly personal relation to things which intrinsically have very little personal appeal for it. It is true that this function of composition is hardly an aesthetic one: for the admiration of mere technical cleverness is not an artistic enjoyment, but by a fortunate chance

99

it has saved from oblivion and entire loss, among much rubbish, also much genuine Art, which otherwise would have completely lost contact with our life.

5. This discussion, necessarily sketchy and incomplete, may have helped to illustrate the sense in which, I suggested, Distance appears as a fundamental principle to which such antitheses as idealism and realism are reducible. The difference between 'idealistic' and 'realistic' Art is not a clear-cut dividing line between the art-practices described by these terms, but is a difference of degree in the Distance-limit which they presuppose on the part both of the artist and of the public. A similar reconciliation seems to me possible between the opposites 'sensual' and 'spiritual,' 'individual' and 'typical.' That the appeal of Art is sensuous, even sensual, must be taken as an indisputable fact. Puritanism will never be persuaded, and rightly so, that this is not the case. The sensuousness of Art is a natural implication of the 'antinomy of Distance,' and will appear again in another connexion. The point of importance here is that the whole sensual side of Art is purified, spiritualised, 'filtered' as I expressed it earlier, by Distance

The most sensual appeal becomes the translucent veil of an underlying spirituality, once the grossly personal and practical elements have been removed from it. And - a matter of special emphasis here - this spiritual aspect of the appeal is the more penetrating, the more personal and direct its sensual appeal would have been BUT FOR THE PRESENCE OF DISTANCE. For the artist, to trust in this delicate transmutation is a natural act of faith which the Puritan hesitates to venture upon: which of the two, one asks, is the greater idealist?

6. The same argument applies to the contradictory epithets 'individual' and 'typical.' A discussion in support of the fundamental individualism of Art lies outside the scope of this essay. Every artist has taken it for granted. Besides it is rather in the sense of 'concrete' or 'individualised,' that it is usually opposed to 'typical.' On the other hand, 'typical,' in the sense of 'abstract,' is as diametrically opposed to the whole nature of Art, as individualism is characteristic of it. It is in the sense of 'generalised' as a 'general human element' that it is claimed as a necessary ingredient

in Art. This antithesis is again one which naturally and without mutual sacrifice finds room within the conception of Distance. Historically the 'typical' has had the effect of counteracting under-distancing as much as the 'individual' has opposed over-distancing. Naturally the two ingredients have constantly varied in the history of Art; they represent, in fact, two sets of conditions to which Art has invariably been subject: the personal and the social factors. It is Distance which on one side prevents the emptying of Art of its concreteness and the development of the typical into abstractness; which, on the other, suppresses the directly personal element of its individualism; thus reducing the antitheses to the peaceful interplay of these two factors. It is just this interplay which constitutes the 'antinomy of Distance.'

III.

It remains to indicate the value of Distance as <u>an aesthetic principle</u>: as criterion in some of the standing problems of Aesthetics; as representing a phase of artistic creation; and as a characteristic feature of the 'aesthetic consciousness.'

102

1. The axiom of 'hedonistic Aesthetics' is that beauty is pleasure. Unfortunately for hedonism the formula is not reversible: not all pleasure is beauty. Hence the necessity of some limiting criterion to separate the beautiful within the 'pleasure-field' from the merely agreeable. This relation of the beautiful to the agreeable is the ever recurring crux of all hedonistic Aesthetics, as the problem of this relation becomes inevitable when once the hedonistic basis is granted. It has provoked a number of widely different solutions, some manifestly wrong, and all as little satisfactory as the whole hedonistic groundwork upon which they rest: the shareableness of beauty as opposed to the 'monopoly' of the agreeable (Bain)[1], the passivity of beauty-pleasure (Grant Allen)[2], or most recently, the 'relative permanence of beauty-pleasure in revival' (H.R. Marshall)[3].

---

1 Bain, The Emotions and the Will, 2nd ed. 1850.
2 G. Allen, Physiological Aesthetics, 1897.
3 H. R. Marshall, Pain, Pleasure and Aesthetics, 1894; Aesthetic Principles, 1895.

Distance offers a distinction which is as simple in its
operation as it is fundamental in its importance: <u>the agreeable
is a non-distanced pleasure.</u> Beauty in the widest sense of
aesthetic value is impossible without the insertion of Distance.
The agreeable stands in precisely the same relation to the
beautiful (in its narrower sense) as the sad stands to the
tragic, as indicated earlier. Translating the above formula,
one may say, that the agreeable is felt as an affection of
our concrete, practical self; the centre of gravity of an
agreeable experience lies in the self which experiences
the agreeable. The aesthetic experience, on the contrary,
has its centre of gravity in itself or in the object
mediating it, not in the self which has been distanced out
of the field of the inner vision of the experiencer:
'not the fruit of experience, but experience itself,
is the end.' It is for this reason that to be asked in
the midst of an intense aesthetic impression 'whether one
likes it,' is like a somnambulist being called by name:
It is a recall to one's concrete self, an awakening of
practical consciousness which throws the whole aesthetic
mechanism out of gear. One might almost venture upon the

paradox that the more intense the aesthetic absorption, the less one 'likes,' consciously, the experience. The failure to realise this fact, so fully borne out by all genuine artistic experience, is the fundamental error of hedonistic Aesthetics.

The problem of the relation of the beautiful and the agreeable has taken more definite shape in the question of the aesthetic value of the so-called 'lower senses' (comprising sensations of taste and temperature, muscular and tactile, and organic sensations). Sight and hearing have always been the 'aesthetic senses' par excellence. Scent has been admitted to the status of an aesthetic sense by some, excluded by others. The ground for the rejection of the lower senses has always been that they mediate only agreeable sensations, but are incapable of conveying aesthetic experiences. Though true normally, this rigid distinction is theoretically unfair to the senses, and in practice often false. It is undoubtedly very difficult to reach an aesthetic appreciation through the lower senses, because the materialness of their action, their proximity and bodily connexion are great obstacles to their distancing.

The aroma of coffee may be a kind of foretaste, taste etherialised, but still a taste. The sweetness of scent of a rose is usually felt more as a bodily caress than as an aesthetic experience. Yet poets have not hesitated to call the scents of flowers their 'souls.' Shelley has transformed the scent to an imperceptible sound.[1] We call such conceptions 'poetical': they mark the transition from the merely agreeable to the beautiful by means of distance.

M. Guyau, in a well-known passage[2], has described the same transformation of a taste. Even muscular sensations may present aesthetic possibilities, in the free exercise of bodily movement, the swing of a runner, in the ease and certainty of the trained gymnast; nay, such diffuse organic sensations as the buoyancy of well-being, and the elasticity of bodily energy, can, in privileged moments, be aesthetically enjoyed. That they admit of no material fixation, such as objects of sight and hearing do, and

---

1 Cf. 'The Sensitive Plant.'
2 M. Guyau, Problemes de l'Esthetique eontemporaine, Paris, 1897, 4me ed. Livre I. chap. VI.

for that reason form no part of Art in the narrower sense; that they exist as aesthetic objects only for the moment and for the single being that enjoys them, is no argument against their aesthetic character. Mere material existence and permanence is no aesthetic criterion.

This is all the more true, as even among the experiences of lasting things, such as are generally accounted to yield aesthetic impressions, the merely agreeable occurs as frequently as the beautiful.

Most people imagine that because they are not colour-blind physically or spiritually, and prefer to live in a coloured world rather than in an engraving, they possess an aesthetic appreciation of colour as such. This is the sort of fallacy which hedonistic art-theories produce, and the lack of an exchange of views on the subject only fosters. Everybody believes that he enjoys colour-and for that matter other things just like anyone else. Yet rather the contrary is the case. By far the greater number, when asked why they like a colour, will answer, that they like it, because it strikes them as warm or cold, stimulating or soothing, heavy or light, they constitute a definite type of colour-appreciation and form about sixty per cent of all persons. The remainder assumes, for the greater part, a different attitude. Colours do not appeal to them as effects (largely organic) upon themselves. Their appreciation attributes to colours a kind of personality: colours are energetic, lively, serious, pensive, melancholic, affectionate, subtle, reserved, stealthy, treacherous, brutal, etc. These characters are not mere imaginings, left to the whim of the individual, romancing whatever he pleases into the colours, nor are they the work simply of accidental associations. They follow, on the contrary, definite rules in their applications; they are, in fact, the same organic effects as those of the former type, but transformed into, or interpreted as, attributes of the colour, instead of as affections of one's own self. In short, they are the result of the distancing of the organic effects: they form an aesthetic appreciation of colour, instead of a merely agreeable experience like those of the former kind.[1]

---

1 Cf. E. Bullough, 'The Perceptive Problem in the Aesthetic Appreciati of Single Colours,' this *Journal*, 1908, II. 406 ff.

A similar parallelism of the agreeable and the beautiful (in the widest sense of aesthetic value) occurs also within the sphere of recognised art-forms. I select for special notice comedy and melodrama (though the same observation can be made in painting, architecture and notably in music), firstly as counterparts to tragedy, discussed earlier, secondly, because both represent admitted art-forms, in spite of their at least partially, inadequate claims to the distinction, and lastly because all these types, tragedy, comedy and melodrama, are usually grouped together as 'arts of the theatre' no less than as forms of 'literature.'

From the point of view of the present discussion, the case of comedy is particularly involved. What we mean by comedy as a class of theatrical entertainment covers several different kinds[1], which actually merge into each

---

1 Comedy embraces satirical comedy, i.e. dramatic invectives of all degrees of personal directness, from the attack on actually existing persons (such as is prohibited by the censorship, but has flourished everywhere) to skits upon existing professions, customs, evils, or society; secondly, farce, rarely unmixed with satire, but occasionally pure nonsense and horseplay; thirdly, comedy proper, a sublimation of farce into

> the pure comedy of general human situation, or genuine
> character-comedy, changing easily into the fourth class,
> the type of play described on the Continent as drama (in
> the narrower sense), i.e. a play involving serious situ-
> ations, sometimes with tragic prospects, but having an
> happy, if often unexpected, ending.

other and present historically a continuity which allows of no

sharp lines of demarcation (a difficulty, by the way, which

besets all distinctions of literary or artistic species, as op-

posed to artistic genera). The second difficulty is that the

'laughable' includes much more than the comic of comedy. It may

enter, in all its varieties of the ridiculous, silly, naïve, brill-

liant, especially as the humorous, into comedy as ingredients,

but the comic is not coextensive with the laughable as a whole.

The fact to be noted here is, that the different types

of comedy, as well as the different kinds of the laughable,

presuppose different degrees of Distance. Their tendency is

to have none at all. Both to laugh and to weep are direct

expressions of a thoroughly practical nature, indicating

almost always a concrete personal affection. Indeed, given

suitable circumstances and adequate distancing-power, both

can be distanced, but only with great difficulty; nor is it

possible to decide which of the two offers the greater

difficulty. The balance seems almost to incline in favour of tears as the easier of the two, and this would accord with the acknowledged difficulty of producing a really good comedy, or of maintaining a consistent aesthetic attitude in face of a comic situation. Certainly the tendency to <u>under</u>distance is more felt in comedy even than in tragedy; most types of the former presenting a <u>non-distanced</u>, practical and personal appeal, which precisely implies that their enjoyment is generally hedonic, not aesthetic. In its lower forms comedy consequently is a mere amusement and falls as little under the heading of Art as pamphleteering would be considered as <u>belles-lettres</u>, or a burglary as a dramatic performance. It may be spiritualised, polished and refined to the sharpness of a dagger-point or the subtlety of foil-play, but there still clings to it an atmosphere of amusement pure and simple, sometimes of a rude, often of a cruel kind. This, together with the admitted preference of comedy for generalised types rather than for individualised figures, suggests the conclusion that its point of view is the survival of an attitude which the higher forms of Art have outgrown.

111

It is noteworthy that this tendency decreases with every step towards high comedy, character-comedy and drama, with the growing spiritualisation of the comic elements and the first appearance of Distance. Historically the development has been slow and halting. There is no doubt that the 17th century considered the Misanthrope as amusing. We are nowadays less harsh and less socially intolerant and Alceste appears to us no longer as frankly ridiculous. The supreme achievement of comedy is unquestionably that 'distanced ridicule' which we call humour. This self-contradiction of smiling at what we love, displays, in the light vein, that same perfect and subtle balance of the 'antinomy of Distance' which the truly tragic shows in the serious mood. The tragic and the humorous are the genuine aesthetic opposites; the tragic and the comic are contradictory in the matter of Distance, as aesthetic and hedonic objects respectively.

A similar hedonic opposition in the other direction is to be found between tragedy and melodrama. Whereas comedy tends to under-distance, melodrama suffers from overdistancing. For a cultivated audience its overcharged

112

idealism, the crude opposition of vice and virtue, the exaggeration of its underlined moral, its innocence of nuance, and its sentimentality with violin-accompaniment are sufficient cause to stamp it as inferior Art. But perhaps its excessive distance is the least Distance obtainable by the public for which it is designed, and may be a great help to an unsophisticated audience in distancing the characters and events. For it is more than probable that we make a mistake in assuming an analogy between a cultivated audience at a serious drama, and a melodramatic audience. It is very likely that the lover of melodrama does not present that subtle balance of mind towards a play, implied in the 'antinomy of Distance.' His attitude is rather either that of a matter-of-fact adult or of a child: i.e. he is either in a frankly personal relation to the events of the play and would like to cudgel the villain who illtreats the innocent heroine, and rejoices loudly in his final defeat - just as he would in real life - or, he is completely lost in the excessive distance imposed by the work and watches naively the wonders he sees, as a child listens enchantedly to a fairy-tale.

In neither case is his attitude aesthetic; in the one the object is under-, in the other overdistanced; in the former he confuses it with the reality he knows (or thinks he knows) to exist, in the other with a reality whose existence he does not know, but accepts. Neither bears the twofold character of the aesthetic state in which we know a thing not to exist, but accept its existence. From the point of view of moral advantage - in the absence of any aesthetic advantage - the former attitude might seem preferable But even this may be doubted; for if he believes what he sees in a great spectacular melodrama, every marble-lined hall of the most ordinary London hotel that he passes after the play must appear to him as a veritable Hell, and every man or woman in evening-dress as the devil incarnate. On either supposition the moral effect must be deplorable in the extreme, and the melodrama is generally a much more fitting object of the censor's attention than any usually censored play. For in the one case the brutalising effect of the obtrusively visible wickedness cannot possibly be outweighed by any retaliatory poetic justice, which must seem to him singularly lacking in real life; in the other, the effect is purely

114

negative and narcotic; in both his perspective of real life is hopelessly outfocussed and distorted.

2. The importance of Distance in artistic creation has already been briefly alluded to in connexion with the 'antinomy of Distance.'

Distancing might, indeed, well be considered as the especial and primary function of what is called the 'creative act' in artistic production: distancing is the formal aspect of creation in Art. The view that the artist 'copies nature' has already been dismissed. Since the 'imitation-of-nature' theory was officially discarded at the beginning of the 19th century, its place in popular fancy has been taken by the conception of the 'self-expression of the artist,' supported by the whole force of the Romantic Movement in Europe. Though true as a crude statement of the subjective origin of an artistic conception, though in many ways preferable to its predecessor and valuable as a corollary of such theories as that of the 'organic growth' of a work of Art, it is apt to lead to confusions and to one-sided inferences, to be found even in such deliberate and expert accounts of artistic production as

115

that of Benedetto Croce[1]. For, to start with, the 'self-expression' of an artist is not such as the 'self-expression' of a letter-writer or a public speaker: it is not the direct expression of the concrete personality of the artist; it is not even an indirect expression of his concrete personality, in the sense in which, for instance, Hamlet's 'self-expression' might be supposed to be the indirect reflexion of Shakespeare's idea. Such a denial, it might be argued, runs counter to the observation that in the works of a literary artist, for example, are to be found echoes and mirrorings of his times and of his personal experiences and convictions. But it is to be noted that to find these is in fact impossible, unless you previously know what reflexions to look for. Even in the relatively most direct transference from personal experiences to their expression, viz. in lyrical poetry, such a connexion cannot be established backwards, though it is easy enough to prove it forwards: i.e. given the knowledge of the experiences, there is no difficulty in tracing their echoes,

---

1 Benedetto Croce, Aesthetic, translated by Douglas Ainslie, Macmillan, 1909.

but it is impossible to infer biographical data of any detail or concrete value from an author's works alone. Otherwise Shakespeare's _Sonnets_ would not have proved as refractory to biographical research as they have done, and endless blunders in literary history would never have been committed. What proves so impossible in literature, which after all offers an exceptionally adequate medium to 'self-expression,' is a _fortiori_ out of question in other arts, in which there is not even an equivalence between the personal experiences and the material in which they are supposed to be formulated. The fundamental two-fold error of the 'self-expression' theory is to speak of 'expression' in the sense of 'intentional communication,' and to identify straightway the artist and the man. An intentional communication is as far almost from the mind of the true artist as it would be from that of the ordinary respectable citizen to walk about naked in the streets, and the idea has repeatedly been indignantly repudiated by artists. The second confusion is as mis-leading in its theoretical consequences, as it is mischievous and often exceedingly painful to the 'man' as well as to the 'artist.' The numberless instances in history of the astonishing difference, often the marked contrast between the man and his work is one of the most disconcerting riddles of Art, and should serve as a manifest warning against the popular illusion of finding the 'artist's mind' in his productions[1].

Apart from the complication of technical necessities, of conventional art-forms, of the requirements of unification and composition, all impeding the direct transference of an actual mental content into its artistic formulation, there is the interpolation of Distance which stands between the artist's conception and the man's. For the 'artist' himself is already distanced from the concrete, historical personality, who ate and drank and slept and did the ordinary business of life. No doubt here also are degrees of Distance, and the 'antinomy' applies to this case too. Some figures in literature and other arts are unquestionably self-portraits; but even self-portraits are not, and cannot be, the direct and faith

---

1 Some well-known examples of this difference are, for instance: Mozart, Beethoven, Watteau, Murillo, Moliere, Schiller, Verlaine, Zola.

ful cast taken from the living soul. In short, so far from being 'self-expression,' artistic production is the indirect formulation of a distanced mental content.

I give a short illustration of this fact. A well-known dramatist described to me the process of production as taking place in his case in some such way as follows:

The starting-point of his production is what he described as an 'emotional idea,' i.e. some more or less general conception carrying with it a strong emotional tone. This idea may be suggested by an actual experience; anyhow the idea itself is an actual experience, i.e. it occurs within the range of his normal, practical being. Gradually it condenses itself into a situation made up of the interplay of certain characters, which may be of partly objective, partly imaginative descent. Then ensues what he described as a 'life and death struggle' between the idea and the characters for existence: if the idea gains the upper hand, the conception of the whole is doomed. In the successful issue, on the contrary, the idea is, to use his phrase, 'sucked up' by the characters as a sponge sucks up water, until no trace of the idea is left outside the characters.

119

It is a process, which, he assured me, he is quite power-
less to direct or even to influence. It is further of
interest to notice that during this period the idea undergoes sometimes profound, often wholesale changes. Once
the stage of complete fusion of the idea with the characters
is reached, the conscious elaboration of the play can
proceed. What follows after this, is of no further
interest in this connexion.

This account tallies closely with the procedure
which numerous dramatists are known to have followed.
It forms a definite type. There are other types, equally
well supported by evidence, which proceed along much less
definite lines of a semi-logical development, but rather
show sudden flash-like illuminations and much more
sub-conscious growth.

The point to notice is the 'life and death struggle'
between the idea and the characters. As I first remarked,
the idea is the 'man's,' it is the reflexion of the
dramatist's concrete and practical self. Yet this is
precisely the part which must 'die.' The paradox of just
the germ-part of the whole being doomed, particularly

120

impressed my informant as a kind of life-tragedy. The 'characters' on the other hand belong to the imaginary world, to the 'artist's.' Though they may be partially suggested by actuality, their full-grown development is divorced from it. This process of the 'idea' being 'sucked up' by the characters and being destroyed by it, is a phase of artistic production technically known as the 'objectivation' of the conception. In it the 'man' dies and the 'artist' comes to life, and with him the work of Art. It is a change of death and birth in which there is no overlapping of the lives of parent and child. The result is the distanced finished production. As elsewhere, the distancing means the separation of personal affections, whether idea or complex experience, from the concrete personality of the experiencer, its filtering by the extrusion of its personal aspects, the throwing out of gear of its personal potency and significance.

The same transformation through distance is to be noticed in _acting_. Here, even more than in the other arts, a lingering bias in favour of the 'imitation of nature' theory has stood in the way of a correct interpretation of the facts. Yet acting supplies in this and other respects exceptionally valuable information, owing to its medium of expression and the overlapping - at least in part - of the process of producing with the finished production, which elsewhere are separated in point of time. It illustrates, as no other art can, the cleavage between the concrete, normal person and the distanced personality. The acting here referred to is, of course, not that style which consists in 'walking on.' What is meant here is 'creative' acting, which in its turn must be distinguished from 'reproductive' acting - two different types traceable through the greater part of theatrical history, which in their highest development are often outwardly indistinguishable, but nevertheless retain traces of differences, characteristic of their procedures and psychical mechanism. This cleavage between the two streams or layers of consciousness is so obvious that it has led to increasing speculation from the time when acting first attracted intelligent interest, since the middle of the 18th century. From the time of Diderot's Paradoxe sur le Comedien (itself only the last

122

of a series of French studies) down to Mr. William Archer's
Masks or Faces (1888) and the controversy between Coquelin
and Salvini (in the nineties), theory has been at pains
to grapple with this phenomenon. Explanations have differed
widely, going from the one extreme of an identification
of the acting and the normal personality to the other of
a separation so wide as to be theoretically inconceivable
and contradicted by experience. It is necessary to offer
some conception which will account for the differences
as well as for the indirect connexion between the two
forms of being, and which is applicable not merely to
acting, but to other kinds of art as well. Distance,
it is here contended, meets the requirement even in its
subtlest shades. To show this in detail lies outside the
scope of this essay, and forms rather the task of a
special treatment of the psychology of acting.

3. In the interest of those who may be familiar
with the developments of aesthetic theories of late years,
I should like to add that Distance has a special bearing
upon many points raised by them. It is essential to the
occurrence and working of 'empathy' (Einfuhlung), and I

mentioned earlier its connexion with Witasek's theory of Scheingefuhle which forms part of his view on 'empathy.' The distinction between sympathy and 'empathy' as formulated by Lipps [1] is a matter of the relative degree of Distance. Volkelt's [2] suggestion of regarding the ordinary apprehension of expression (say of a person's face) as the first rudimentary stage of Einfuhlung, leading subsequently to the lowering of our consciousness of reality ('Herabsetzung des Wirklichkeitsgefuhls'), can similarly be formulated in terms of Distance. K. Lange's [3] account of aesthetic experience in the form of 'illusion as conscious self-deception' appears to me a wrong formulation of the facts expressed by Distance. Lange's 'illusion' theory seems to me, among other things, [4] to be based upon a false opposition between Art and reality (nature) as the subject-matter of the former, whereas Distance does not imply any comparison between

1 Th. Lipps, Aesthetik, Hamburg and Leipzig, 1903, I; 'Aesthetische Einfuhlung,' Ztsch. fur Psychol. u. Physiol. der Sinnesorg, XXII. 415 ff.
2 J. Volkelt, System der Aesthetik, 1905, I. 217 ff. and 488 ff.
3 K. Lange, Des Wesen der Kunst, 1901, 2 vols.
4 J. Segal, 'Die bewusste Selbsttauschung als Kern des aesthetischen Geniessens Arch. f. d. ges. Psychol. VI. 254 ff.

them in the act of experiencing and removes altogether the centre of gravity of the formula from the opposition.

4. In this way Distance represents in aesthetic appreciation as well as in artistic production a quality inherent in the impersonal, yet so intensely personal, relation which the human being entertains with Art, either as mere beholder or as producing artist.

It is Distance which makes the aesthetic object 'an end in itself.' It is that which raises Art beyond the narrow sphere of individual interest and imparts to it that 'postulating' character which the idealistic philosophy of the 19th century regarded as a metaphysical necessity. It renders questions of origin, of influences, or of purposes almost as meaningless as those of marketable value, of pleasure, even of moral importance, since it lifts the work of Art out of the realm of practical systems and ends.

In particular, it is Distance, which supplies one of the special criteria of aesthetic values as distinct from practical (utilitarian), scientific, or social (ethical) values. All these are concrete values, either directly

125

personal as utilitarian, or indirectly remotely personal,
as moral values. To speak, therefore, of the 'pleasure
value' of Art, and to introduce hedonism into aesthetic
speculation, is even more irrelevant than to speak of moral
hedonism in Ethics. Aesthetic hedonism is a compromise.
It is the attempt to reconcile for public use utilitarian
ends with aesthetic values. Hedonism, as a practical,
personal appeal has no place in the distanced appeal of
Art. Moral Hedonism is even more to the point than aesthetic
hedonism, since ethical values, qua social values, lie on
the line of prolongation of utilitarian ends, sublimating
indeed the directly personal object into the realm of
socially or universally valuable ends, often demanding
the sacrifice of individual happiness, but losing neither
its practical nor even its remotely personal character.

In so far, Distance becomes one of the distinguishing
features of the 'aesthetic consciousness,' of that special
mentality or outlook upon experience and life, which, as
I said at the outset, leads in its most pregnant and most
fully developed form, both appreciatively and productively,
to Art."

AESTHETIC EXPERIENCE AS CLARIFIED AND INTENSIFIED EXPERIENCE

Dewey's treatment of aesthetic experience is an immensely rich contribution from which subsequent aestheticians have greatly benefited. Nevertheless, it must be noted that Dewey does not excel in tightness of organization, nor is he given to economy of statement, and, at times, he is lacking in specificity. But some of his suggestive power probably hinges upon a loose, rambling style and would be lost in a terse, precise, point-by-point analysis. The reader, however, is apt to derive more from Dewey's exposition if the following matters are kept in mind. In the present selection, Dewey uses the word "experience" in three different senses. Sometimes he speaks of what is called normal or ordinary experience; this serves as a foil for his second and cardinal conception which he terms an experience. Third, and less often, he talks about experiences which are dominantly aesthetic. These various senses must be fully understood if Dewey's message is to be grasped and evaluated.

First, let us examine what he tells us about ordinary

or normal experiences. They are all potentially aesthetic, for Dewey states (in Chapter one of <u>Art as Experience</u>) that aesthetic quality is present implicitly in any normal experience. Normal experiences are said to be inchoate in contrast to <u>an experience</u>. Ordinary experiences are choppy, interrupted, dispersed. Dewey points out that in such experiences we do not attend to the connection of one event with what preceded it or with what follows it. Things occur, but they are not apprehended as constituents of a single, intact experience. Aesthetic quality is implicit but unrealized in ordinary experiences or happenings.

Second, in <u>an experience,</u> " . . . the material experienced runs its course to fulfillment." Various ingredients are rounded out so as to reach a consummation. <u>An experience</u> always possesses unity; and, Dewey holds that no experience is unified without having aesthetic quality. The unity of <u>an experience</u> is constituted by a pervading aesthetic quality. Aesthetic quality is that which "rounds out an experience into completeness and unity . . ." <u>An experience</u>, therefore, always has explicit aesthetic

128

quality as contrasted with ordinary experiences in which aesthetic quality is only implicit.

Finally, Dewey also distinguishes between <u>an experience</u> and aesthetic experience in the fullfledged sense. In the former, the experience is aesthetic in quality, character, or tone. In the latter, which Dewey terms a dominantly aesthetic experience, there is a counterpart for what we earlier called a wholly aesthetic experience, for the development of such distinctively aesthetic experiences is in no way controlled by the practical or intellectual interests which operate in the case of <u>an experience.</u> This last sort of experience underlines the trans-practical, non-utilitarian aspect of aesthetic experiences.

From the above, it is obvious that Dewey gives preeminence to the trans-chaotic or unitary character of the aesthetic. His concentration is upon what we have named sequential unity or the unity of continuity as distinguished from the unity of equilibrium. He also recognizes the trans-mundane feature of the aesthetic when he tells us that <u>an experience </u>is the sort of thing about which we say: "Now, that was an experience."

Our meaning here would be that it stood out from run-of-the-mill experiences. If an experience is extraordinary, so much the more will be the aesthetic experience from which all practical and intellectual considerations have been abstracted.

Because Dewey is a naturalist, it is predictable that the aesthetic rather than the spiritual will become his supreme category of experience. A religiously-oriented person, on the other hand, might be prone to substitute the religious for the aesthetic in order to designate the omnipresent quality inherent in all normal experiences. Unity, integration, movement toward consummation could all be interpreted spiritually, perhaps mystically. Dewey's theory has been attacked on the grounds that it does not do justice to the break from the ordinary which is characteristic of aesthetic experiences. But, as we have seen, he definitely does mark off an experience and distinctively aesthetic experiences from ordinary experiences. In the end, what is most noteworthy is that such demarcation is not so absolute as to interfere with Dewey's announced goal: to restore the continuity between art and life.

HAVING AN EXPERIENCE

"Experience occurs continuously, because the interaction of
live creature and environing conditions is involved in the very
process of living. Under conditions of resistance and conflict, aspects and elements of the self and the world that
are implicated in this interaction qualify experience with
emotions and ideas so that conscious intent emerges. Often-
times, however, the experience had is inchoate. Things are
experienced but not in such a way that they are composed
into _an_ experience. There is distraction and dispersion;
what we observe and what we think, what we desire and what
we get, are at odds with each other. We put our hands to
the plow and turn back; we start and then we stop, not because
the experience has reached the end for the sake of which
it was initiated but because of extraneous interruptions or
of innner lethargy.

In contrast with such experience, we have _an_ experience
when the material experienced runs its course to fulfillment.
Then and then only is it integrated within and demarcated in
the general stream of experience from other experiences. A

piece of work is finished in a way that is satisfactory;
a problem receives its solution; a game is played through;
a situation, whether that of eating a meal, playing a
game of chess, carrying on a conversation, writing a
book, or taking part in a political campaign, is so
rounded out that its close is a consummation and not a
cessation. Such an experience is a whole and carries
with it its own individualizing quality and self-sufficiency.
It is an experience.

Philosophers, even empirical philosophers, have spoken
for the most part of experience at large. Idiomatic speech,
however, refers to experiences each of which is singular,
having its own beginning and end. For life is no uniform
uninterrupted march or flow. It is a thing of histories,
each with its own plot, its own inception and movement
toward its close, each having its own particular rhythmic
movement; each with its own unrepeated quality pervading
it throughout. A flight of stairs, mechanical as it is,
proceeds by individualized steps, not by undifferentiated
progression, and an inclined plane is at least marked off
from other things by abrupt discreteness.

Experience in this vital sense is defined by those situations and episodes that we spontaneously refer to as being 'real experiences'; those things of which we say in recalling them, 'that _was_ an experience.' It may have been something of tremendous importance - a quarrel with one who was once an intimate, a catastrophe finally averted by a hair's breadth. Or it may have been something that in comparison was slight - and which perhaps because of its very slightness illustrates all the better what is to be an experience. There is that meal in a Paris restaurant of which one says 'that _was_ an experience.' It stands out as an enduring memorial of what food may be. Then there is that storm one went through in crossing the Atlantic - the storm that seemed in its fury, as it was experienced, to sum up in itself all that a storm can be, complete in itself, standing out because marked out from what went before and what came after.

In such experiences, every successive part flows freely, without seam and without unfilled blanks, into what ensues. At the same time there is no sacrifice of

the self-identity of the parts. A river, as distinct
from a pond, flows. But its flow gives a definiteness
and interest to its successive portions greater than
exist in the homogenous portions of a pond. In an
experience, flow is from something to something. As
one part leads into another and as one part carries on
what went before, each gains distinctness in itself.
The enduring whole is diversified by successive phases
that are emphases of its varied colors.

Because of continuous merging, there are no holes,
mechanical junctions, and dead centers when we have an
experience. There are pauses, places of rest, but they
punctuate and define the quality of movement. They sum
up what has been undergone and prevent its dissipation
and idle evaporation. Continued acceleration is breathless
and prevents parts from gaining distinction. In a work
of art different acts, episodes, occurrences melt and
fuse into unity, and yet do not disappear and lose
their own character as they do so - just as in a genial
conversation there is a continuous interchange and blending,
and yet each speaker not only retains his own character

134

but manifests it more clearly than is his wont.

An experience has a unity that gives it its name, that meal, that storm, that rupture of friendship. The existence of this unity is constituted by a single quality that pervades the entire experience in spite of the variation of its constituent parts. This unity is neither emotional, practical, nor intellectual, for these terms name distinctions that reflection can make within it. In discourse about an experience, we must make use of these adjectives of interpretation. In going over an experience in mind after its occurrence, we may find that one property rather than another was sufficiently dominant so that it characterizes the experience as a whole. There are absorbing inquiries and speculations which a scientific man and philosopher will recall as 'experiences' in the emphatic sense. In final import they are intellectual. But in their actual occurrence they were emotional as well; they were purposive and volitional. Yet the experience was not a sum of these different characters; they were lost in it as distinctive traits. No thinker can ply his occupation save as he is lured and rewarded by total integral experiences that are

intrinsically worthwhile. Without them he would never know
what it is really to think and would be completely at a
loss in distinguishing real thought from the spurious
article. Thinking goes on in trains of ideas, but the
ideas form a train only because they are much more than
what an analytic psychology calls ideas. They are phases,
emotionally and practically distinguished, of a developing
underlying quality; they are its moving variations, not
separate and independent like Locke's and Hume's so called
ideas and impressions, but are subtle shadings of a
pervading and developing hue.

We say of an experience of thinking that we reach or
draw a conclusion. Theoretical formulation of the process
is often made in such terms as to conceal effectually the
similarity of 'conclusion' to the consummating phase of every
developing integral experience. These formulations apparently
take their cue from the separate propositions that are
premisses and the proposition that is the conclusion as they
appear on the printed page. The impression is derived that
there are first two independent and ready-made entities that
are then manipulated so as to give rise to a third. In fact,

in an experience of thinking, premisses emerge only as a conclusion becomes manifest. The experience, like that of watching a storm reach its height and gradually subside, is one of continuous movement of subject-matters. Like the ocean in the storm, there are a series of waves; suggestions reaching out and being broken in a clash, or being carried onwards by a cooperative wave. If a conclusion is reached, it is that of a movement of anticipation and cumulation, one that finally comes to completion. A 'conclusion' is no separate and independent thing; it is the consummation of a movement.

Hence an experience of thinking has its own esthetic quality. It differs from those experiences that are acknowledged to be esthetic, but only in its materials. The material of the fine arts consists of qualities; that of experience having intellectual conclusion are signs or symbols having no intrinsic quality of their own, but standing for things that may in another experience be qualitatively experienced. The difference is enormous. It is one reason why the strictly intellectual art will never be popular as music is popular. Nevertheless, the

experience itself has a satisfying emotional quality
because it possesses internal integration and fulfillment
reached through ordered and organized movement. This
artistic structure may be immediately felt. In so far,
it is esthetic. What is even more important is that
not only is this quality a significant motive in undertaking intellectual inquiry and in keeping it honest,
but that no intellectual activity is an integral event
(is an _experience_), unless it is rounded out with this
quality. Without it, thinking is inconclusive. In
short, esthetic cannot be sharply marked off from intellectual
experience since the latter must bear an esthetic stamp
to be itself complete.

The same statement holds good of a course of action
that is dominantly practical, that is, one that consists
of overt doings. It is possible to be efficient in action
and yet not have a conscious experience. The activity is
too automatic to permit of a sense of what it is about and
where it is going. It comes to an end but not to a close
or consummation in consciousness. Obstacles are overcome
by shrewd skill, but they do not feed experience. There

138

are also those who are wavering in action, uncertain, and inconclusive like the shades in classic literature. Between the poles of aimlessness and mechanical efficiency, there lie those courses of action in which through successive deeds there runs a sense of growing meaning conserved and accumulating toward an end that is felt as accomplishment of a process. Successful politicians and generals who turn statesmen like Caesar and Napoleon have something of the showman about them. This of itself is not art, but it is, I think, a sign that interest is not exclusively, perhaps not mainly, held by the result taken by itself (as it is in the case of mere efficiency), but by it as the outcome of a process. There is interest in completing an experience. The experience may be one that is harmful to the world and its consummation undesirable. But it has esthetic quality.

The Greek identification of good conduct with conduct having proportion, grace, and harmony, the kalon-agathon, is a more obvious example of distinctive esthetic quality in moral action. One great defect in what passes as morality is its anesthetic quality. Instead of exemplifying

139

wholehearted action, it takes the form of grudging piecemeal concessions to the demands of duty. But illustrations may only obscure the fact that any practical activity will, provided that it is integrated and moves by its own urge to fulfillment, have esthetic quality.

A generalized illustration may be had if we imagine a stone, which is rolling down hill, to have an experience. The activity is surely sufficiently 'practical.' The stone starts from somewhere, and moves, as consistently as conditions permit, toward a place and state where it will be at rest - toward an end. Let us add, by imagination, to these external facts, the ideas that it looks forward with desire to the final outcome; that it is interested in the things it meets on its way, conditions that accelerate and retard its movement with respect to their bearing on the end; that it acts and feels toward them according to the hindering or helping function it attributes to them; and that the final coming to rest is related to all that went before as the culmination of a continuous movement. Then the stone would have an experience, and one with esthetic quality.

140

If we turn from this imaginary case to our own experience, we shall find much of it is nearer to what happens to the actual stone than it is to anything that fulfills the conditions fancy just laid down. For in much of our experience we are not concerned with the connection of one incident with what went before and what comes after. There is no interest that controls attentive rejection or selection of what shall be organized into the developing experience. Things happen, but they are neither definitely included nor decisively excluded; we drift. We yield according to external pressure, or evade and compromise. There are beginnings and cessations, but no genuine initiations and concludings. One thing replaces another, but does not absorb it and carry it on. There is experience, but so slack and discursive that it is not an experience. Needless to say, such experiences are anesthetic.

Thus the non-esthetic lies within two limits. At one pole is the loose succession that does not begin at any particular place and that ends - in the sense of ceasing - at no particular place. At the other pole is arrest, constriction, proceeding from parts having only

a mechanical connection with one another. There exists
so much of one and the other of these two kinds of
experience that unconsciously they come to be taken as
norms of experience. Then, when the esthetic appears,
it so sharply contrasts with the picture that has been
formed of experience, that it is impossible to combine
its special qualities with the features of the picture
and the esthetic is given an outside place and status.
The account that has been given of experience dominantly
intellectual and practical is intended to show that
there is no such contrast involved in having an experience;
that, on the contrary, no experience of whatever sort
is a unity unless it has esthetic quality.

The enemies of the esthetic are neither the practical
nor the intellectual. They are the humdrum; slackness
of loose ends; submission to convention in practice
and intellectual procedure. Rigid abstinence, coerced
submission, tightness on one side and dissipation,
incoherence and aimless indulgence on the other, are
deviations in opposite directions from the unity of an
experience. Some such considerations perhaps induced

142

Aristotle to invoke the 'mean proportional' as the proper designation of what is distinctive of both virtue and the esthetic. He was formally correct. 'Mean' and 'proportion' are, however, not self-explanatory, nor to be taken over in a prior mathematical sense, but are properties belonging to an experience that has a developing movement toward its own consummation.

I have emphasized the fact that every integral experience moves toward a close, an ending, since it ceases only when the energies active in it have done their proper work. This closure of a circuit of energy is the opposite of arrest, of stasis. Maturation and fixation are polar opposites. Struggle and conflict may be themselves enjoyed, although they are painful, when they are experienced as means of developing an experience; members in that they carry it forward, not just because they are there. There is, as will appear later, an element of undergoing, of suffering in its large sense, in every experience. Otherwise there would be no taking in of what preceded. For 'taking in' in any vital experience is something more than placing something on the top of

consciousness over what was previously known. It involves
reconstruction which may be painful. Whether the necessary
undergoing phase is by itself pleasurable or painful is a
matter of particular conditions. It is indifferent to
the total esthetic quality, save that there are few intense
esthetic experiences that are wholly gleeful. They are
certainly not to be characterized as amusing, and as they
bear down upon us they involve a suffering that is none
the less consistent with, indeed a part of, the complete
perception that is enjoyed.

I have spoken of the esthetic quality that rounds out
an experience into completeness and unity as emotional.
The reference may cause difficulty. We are given to
thinking of emotions as things as simple and compact
as are the words by which we name them. Joy, sorrow,
hope, fear, anger, curiosity, are treated as if each in
itself were a sort of entity that enters full-made
upon the scene, an entity that may last a long time or a
short time, but whose duration, whose growth and career,
is irrelevant to its nature. In fact emotions are
qualities, when they are significant, of a complex

144

experience that moves and changes. I say, when they are significant, for otherwise they are but the outbreaks and eruptions of a disturbed infant. All emotions are qualifications of a drama and they change as the drama develops. Persons are sometimes said to fall in love at first sight. But what they fall into is not a thing of that instant. What would love be were it compressed into a moment in which there is no room for cherishing and for solicitude? The intimate nature of emotion is manifested in the experience of one watching a play on the stage or reading a novel. It attends the development of a plot; and a plot requires a stage, a space, wherein to develop and time in which to unfold. Experience is emotional but there are no separate things called emotions in it.

By the same token, emotions are attached to events and objects in their movement. They are not, save in pathological instances, private. And even an 'objectless' emotion demands something beyond itself to which to attach itself, and thus it soon generates a delusion in lack of something real. Emotion belongs of a certainty to the self. But it belongs to the self that is concerned in the movement

of events toward an issue that is desired or disliked.
We jump instantaneously when we are scared, as we blush
on the instant when we are ashamed. But fright and shamed
modesty are not in this case emotional states. Of
themselves they are but automatic reflexes. In order to
become emotional they must become parts of an inclusive
and enduring situation that involves concern for objects
and their issues. The jump of fright becomes emotional
fear when there is found or thought to exist a threatening
object that must be dealt with or escaped from. The blush
becomes the emotion of shame when a person connects, in
thought, an action he has performed with an unfavorable
reaction to himself of some other person.

Physical things from far ends of the earth are physically
transported and physically caused to act and react upon
one another in the construction of a new object. The miracle
of mind is that something similar takes place in experience
without physical transport and assembling. Emotion is the
moving and cementing force. It selects what is congruous
and dyes what is selected with its color, thereby giving
qualitative unity to materials externally disparate and

146

dissimilar. It thus provides unity in and through the varied parts of an experience. When the unity is of the sort already described, the experience has esthetic character even though it is not, dominantly, an esthetic experience.

Two men meet; one is the applicant for a position, while the other has the disposition of the matter in his hands. The interview may be mechanical, consisting of set questions, the replies to which perfunctorily settle the matter. There is no experience in which the two men meet, nothing that is not a repetition, by way of acceptance or dismissal, of something which has happened a score of times. The situation is disposed of as if it were an exercise in bookkeeping. But an interplay may take place in which a new experience develops. Where should we look for an account of such an experience? Not to ledger-entries nor yet to a treatise on economics or sociology or personnel-psychology, but to drama or fiction. Its nature and import can be expressed only by art, because there is a unity of experience that can be expressed only as an experience. The experience is of

147

material fraught with suspense and moving toward its own
consummation through a connected series of varied incidents.
The primary emotions on the part of the applicant may be
at the beginning hope or despair, and elation or disappoint-
ment at the close. These emotions qualify the experience
as a unity. But as the interview proceeds, secondary
emotions are evolved as variations of the primary underlying one. It is even possible for each attitude and
gesture, each sentence, almost every word, to produce
more than a fluctuation in the intensity of the basic
emotion; to produce, that is, a change of shade and tint
in its quality. The employer sees by means of his own
emotional reactions the character of the one applying.
He projects him imaginatively into the work to be done
and judges his fitness by the way in which the elements
of the scene assemble and either clash or fit together.
The presence and behavior of the applicant either harmonize
with his own attitudes and desires or they conflict and
jar. Such factors as these, inherently esthetic in
quality, are the forces that carry the varied elements
of the interview to a decisive issue. They enter into

the settlement of every situation, whatever its dominant nature, in which there are uncertainty and suspense.

There are, therefore, common patterns in various experiences, no matter how unlike they are to one another in the details of their subject matter. There are conditions to be met without which an experience cannot come to be. The outline of the common pattern is set by the fact that every experience is the result of interaction between a live creature and some aspect of the world in which he lives. A man does something; he lifts, let us say, a stone. In consequence he undergoes, suffers, something: the weight, strain, texture of the surface of the thing lifted. The properties thus undergone determine further doing. The stone is too heavy or too angular, not solid enough; or else the properties undergone show it is fit for the use for which it is intended. The process continues until a mutual adaptation of the self and the object emerges and that particular experience comes to a close. What is true of this simple instance is true, as to form, of every experience. The creature operating may be a thinker in his study and the environment with

149

which he interacts may consist of ideas instead of a
stone. But interaction of the two constitutes the total
experience that is had, and the close which completes it
is the institution of a felt harmony.

An experience has pattern and structure, because it
is not just doing and undergoing in alternation, but consists
of them in relationship. To put one's hand in the fire
that consumes it is not necessarily to have an experience.
The action and its consequence must be joined in perception.
This relationship is what gives meaning; to grasp it is
the objective of all intelligence. The scope and content
of the relations measure the significant content of an
experience. A child's experience may be intense, but,
because of lack of background from past experience,
relations between undergoing and doing are slightly
grasped, and the experience does not have great depth
or breadth. No one ever arrives at such maturity that
he perceives all the connections that are involved.
There was once written (by Mr. Hinton) a romance called
'The Unlearner.' It portrayed the whole endless duration
of life after death as a living over of the incidents

that happened in a short life on earth, in continued discovery of the relationships involved among them.

Experience is limited by all the causes which interfere with perception of the relations between undergoing and doing. There may be interference because of excess on the side of doing or of excess on the side of receptivity, of undergoing. Unbalance on either side blurs the perception of relations and leaves the experience partial and distorted, with scant or false meaning. Zeal for doing, lust for action, leaves many a person, especially in this hurried and impatient human environment in which we live, with experience of an almost incredible paucity, all on the surface. No one experience has a chance to complete itself because something else is entered upon so speedily. What is called experience becomes so dispersed and miscellaneous as hardly to deserve the name. Resistance is treated as an obstruction to be beaten down, not as an invitation to reflection. An individual comes to seek, unconsciously even more than by deliberate choice, situations in which he can do the most things in the shortest time.

Experiences are also cut short from maturing by excess

of receptivity. What is prized is then the mere undergoing
of this and that, irrespective of perception of any meaning.
The crowding together of as many impressions as possible
is thought to be 'life,' even though no one of them is more
than a flitting and a sipping. The sentimentalist and the
day-dreamer may have more fancies and impressions pass
through their consciousness than has the man who is animated
by lust for action. But his experience is equally distorted,
because nothing takes root in mind when there is no balance
between doing and receiving. Some decisive action is
needed in order to establish contact with the realities
of the world and in order that impressions may be so
related to facts that their value is tested and organized.

Because perception of relationship between what is done
and what is undergone constitutes the work of intelligence,
and because the artist is controlled in the process of his
work by his grasp of the connection between what he has
already done and what he is to do next, the idea that the
artist does not think as intently and penetratingly as a
scientific inquirer is absurd. A painter must consciously
undergo the effect of his every brush stroke or he will

152

not be aware of what he is doing and where his work is going. Moreover, he has to see each particular connection of doing and undergoing in relation to the whole that he desires to produce. To apprehend such relations is to think, and is one of the most exacting modes of thought. The difference between the pictures of different painters is due quite as much to differences of capacity to carry on this thought as it is to differences of sensitivity to bare color and to differences in dexterity of execution. As respects the basic quality of pictures, difference depends, indeed, more upon the quality of intelligence brought to bear upon perception of relations than upon anything else - though of course intelligence cannot be separated from direct sensitivity and is connected, though in a more external manner, with skill.

Any idea that ignores the necessary role of intelligence in production of works of art is based upon identification of thinking with use of one special kind of material, verbal signs and words. To think effectively in terms of relations of qualities is as severe a demand upon thought as to think in terms of symbols, verbal and mathematical.

Indeed, since words are easily manipulated in mechanical ways, the production of a work of genuine art probably demands more intelligence than does most of the so-called thinking that goes on among those who pride themselves on being 'intellectuals.'

I have tried to show in these chapters that the esthetic is no intruder in experience from without, whether by way of idle luxury of transcendent ideality, but that it is the clarified and intensified development of traits that belong to every normally complete experience. This fact I take to be the only secure basis upon which esthetic theory can build. It remains to suggest some of the implications of the underlying fact.

We have no word in the English language that unambiguously includes what is signified by the two words 'artistic' and 'esthetic.' Since 'artistic' refers primarily to the act of production and 'esthetic' to that of perception and enjoyment, the absence of a term designating the two processes taken together is unfortunate. Sometimes, the effect is to separate the two from each other, to regard art as something superimposed upon esthetic material, or, upon the other side, to an assumption that, since art is a process of creation, perception and enjoyment of it have nothing in common with the creative act. In any case, there is a certain verbal awkwardness in that we are compelled sometimes to use the term 'esthetic' to cover the entire field and sometimes to limit it to the receiving perceptual aspect of the whole operation. I refer to these obvious facts as preliminary to an attempt to show how the conception of experience as a perceived relation between doing and undergoing enables us to understand the connection that art as production and perception and appreciation as enjoyment sustain to each other.

Art denotes a process of doing or making. This is as true of fine as of technological art. Art involves molding of clay, chipping of marble, casting of bronze, laying on of pigments, construction of buildings, singing of songs, playing of instruments, enacting roles on the stage, going through rhythmic movements in the dance. Every art does something with some physical material, the

155

body or something outside the body, with or without the
use of intervening tools, and with a view to production
of something visible, audible, or tangible. So marked is
the active or 'doing' phase of art, that the dictionaries
usually define it in terms of skilled action, ability
in execution. The Oxford Dictionary illustrates by a
quotation from John Stuart Mill: 'Art is an endeavor
after perfection in execution' while Matthew Arnold calls it
'pure and flawless workmanship.'

The word 'esthetic' refers, as we have already noted,
to experience as appreciative, perceiving, and enjoying.
It denotes the consumer's rather than the producer's
standpoint. It is Gusto, taste; and, as with cooking,
overt skillful action is on the side of the cook who
prepares, while taste is on the side of the consumer, as
in gardening there is a distinction between the gardener
who plants and tills and the householder who enjoys the
finished product.

These very illustrations, however, as well as the
relation that exists in having an experience between doing
and undergoing, indicate that the distinction between esthetic

and artistic cannot be pressed so far as to become a
separation. Perfection in execution cannot be measured
or defined in terms of execution; it implies those who
perceive and enjoy the product that is executed. The
cook prepares food for the consumer and the measure of
the value of what is prepared is found in consumption.
Mere perfection in execution, judged in its own terms in
isolation, can probably be attained better by a machine
than by human art. By itself, it is at most technique,
and there are great artists who are not in the first
ranks as technicians (witness Cezanne), just as there
are great performers on the piano who are not great
esthetically, and as Sargent is not a great painter.

Craftsmanship to be artistic in the final sense must
be 'loving'; it must care deeply for the subject matter
upon which skill is exercised. A sculptor comes to mind
whose busts are marvelously exact. It might be difficult
to tell in the presence of a photograph of one of them
and of a photograph of the original which was of the person
himself. For virtuosity they are remarkable. But one
doubts whether the maker of the busts had an experience

157

of his own that he was concerned to have those share who look at his products. To be truly artistic, a work must also be esthetic - that is, framed for enjoyed receptive perception. Constant observation is, of course, necessary for the maker while he is producing. But if his perception is not also esthetic in nature, it is a colorless and cold recognition of what has been done, used as a stimulus to the next step in a process that is essentially mechanical.

In short, art, in its form, unites the very same relation of doing and undergoing, outgoing and incoming energy, that makes an experience to be an experience. Because of elimination of all that does not contribute to mutual organization of the factors of both action and reception into one another, and because of selection of just the aspects and traits that contribute to their interpenetration of each other, the product is a work of esthetic art. Man whittles, carves, sings, dances, gestures, molds, draws and paints. The doing or making is artistic when the perceived result is of such a nature that its qualities as perceived have controlled the question of production. The act of producing that is directed by intent to produce

158

something that is enjoyed in the immediate experience of perceiving has qualities that a spontaneous or uncontrolled activity does not have. The artist embodies in himself the attitude of the perceiver while he works.

Suppose, for the sake of illustration, that a finely wrought object, one whose texture and proportions are highly pleasing in perception, has been believed to be a product of some primitive people. Then there is discovered evidence that proves it to be an accidental natural product. As an external thing, it is now precisely what it was before. Yet at once it ceases to be a work of art and becomes a natural "curiousity." It now belongs in a museum of natural history, not in a museum of art. And the extraordinary thing is that the difference that is thus made is not one of just intellectual classification. A difference is made in appreciative perception and in a direct way. The esthetic experience - in its limited sense - is thus seen to be inherently connected with the experience of making.

The sensory satisfaction of eye and ear, when esthetic, is so because it does not stand by itself but is linked to the activity of which it is the consequence. Even the

pleasures of the palate are different in quality to an
epicure than in one who merely 'likes' his food as he eats
it. The difference is not of mere intensity. The epicure
is conscious of much more than the taste of the food.
Rather, there enter into the taste, as directly experienced,
qualities that depend upon reference to its source and its
manner of production in connection with criteria of excellence.
As production must absorb into itself qualities of the product
as perceived and be regulated by them, so, on the other side,
seeing, hearing, tasting, become esthetic when relation to a
distinct manner of activity qualifies what is perceived.

There is an element of passion in all esthetic
perception. Yet when we are overwhelmed by passion, as
in extreme rage, fear, jealousy, the experience is definitely
non-esthetic. There is no relationship felt to the
qualities of the activity that has generated the passion.
Consequently, the material of the experience lacks elements
of balance and proportion. For these can be present only
when, as in the conduct that has grace or dignity, the act
is controlled by an exquisite sense of the relations which

160

the act sustains - its fitness to the occasion and to the situation.

The process of art in production is related to the esthetic in perception organically - as the Lord God in creation surveyed his work and found it good. Until the artist is satisfied in perception with what he is doing, he continues shaping and reshaping. The making comes to an end when its result is experienced as good - and that experience comes not by mere intellectual and outside judgment but in direct perception. An artist, in comparison with his fellows, is one who is not only especially gifted in powers of execution but in unusual sensitivity to the qualities of things. This sensitivity also directs his doings and makings.

As we manipulate, we touch and feel, as we look, we see; as we listen, we hear. The hand moves with etching needle or with brush. The eye attends and reports the consequence of what is done. Because of this intimate connection, subsequent doing is cumulative and not a matter of caprice nor yet of routine. In an emphatic artistic esthetic experience, the relation is so close that it

161

controls simultaneously both the doing and the perception.
Such vital intimacy of connection cannot be had if only hand
and eye are engaged. When they do not, both of them, act
as organs of the whole being, there is but a mechanical
sequence of sense and movement, as in walking that is
automatic. Hand and eye, when the experience is esthetic,
are but instruments through which the entire live creature,
moved and active throughout, operates. Hence the expression
is emotional and guided by purpose.

Because of the relation between what is done and
what is undergone, there is an immediate sense of things
in perception as belonging together or as jarring; as
reenforcing or as interfering. The consequences of the
act of making as reported in sense show whether what
is done carries forward the idea being executed or marks
a deviation and break. In as far as the development of
an experience is controlled through reference to these
immediately felt relations of order and fulfillment, that
experience becomes dominantly esthetic in nature. The
urge to action becomes an urge to that kind of action which
will result in an object satisfying in direct perception.

162

The potter shapes his clay to make a bowl useful for holding grain; but he makes it in a way so regulated by the series of perceptions that sum up the serial acts of making, that the bowl is marked by enduring grace and charm. The general situation remains the same in painting a picture or molding a bust. Moreover, at each stage there is anticipation of what is to come. This anticipation is the connecting link between the next doing and its outcome for sense. What is done and what is undergone are thus reciprocally, cumulatively, and continuously instrumental to each other.

The doing may be energetic, and the undergoing may be acute and intense. But unless they are related to each other to form a whole in perception, the thing done is not fully esthetic. The making for example may be a display of technical virtuosity, and the undergoing a gush of sentiment or a revery. If the artist does not perfect a new vision in his process of doing, he acts mechanically and repeats some old model fixed like a blue print in his mind. An incredible amount of observation and of the kind of intelligence that is exercised in perception of qualitative relations characterizes creative work in art. The relations must be noted not only with respect to one another, two by two, but in connection with the whole under construction; they are exercised in imagination as well as in observation. Irrelevancies arise that are tempting distractions; digressions suggest themselves in the guise of enrichments. There are occasions when the grasp of the dominant idea grows faint, and then the artist is moved unconsciously to fill in until his thought grows strong again. The real work of an artist is to build up an experience that is coherent in perception while moving with constant change in its development.

When an author puts on paper ideas that are already clearly conceived and consistently ordered, the real work has been previously done. Or, he may depend upon the greater perceptibility induced by the activity and its sensible report to direct his completion of the work. The mere act of transcription is esthetically irrelevant save as it enters integrally into the formation of an experience moving to completeness. Even the composition conceived in the head and, therefore, physically private,

164

is public in its significant content, since it is conceived with reference to execution in a product that is perceptible and hence belongs to the common world. Otherwise it would be an aberration or a passing dream. The urge to express through painting the perceived qualities of a landscape is continuous with demand for pencil or brush. Without external embodiment, an experience remains incomplete; physiologically and functionally, sense organs are motor organ and are connected, by means of distribution of energies in the human body and not merely anatomically, with other motor organs. It is no linguistic accident that 'building,' 'construction,' 'work,' designate both a process and its finished product. Without the meaning of the verb that of the noun remains blank.

Writer, composer of music, sculptor, or painter can retrace, during the process of production, what they have previously done. When it is not satisfactory in the undergoing or perceptual phase of experience, they can to some degree start afresh. This retracing is not readily accomplished in the case of architecture - which is perhaps one reason why there are so many ugly buildings. Architects

are obliged to complete their idea before its translation
into a complete object of perception takes place. Inability
to build up simultaneously the idea and its objective
embodiment imposes a handicap. Nevertheless, they too
are obliged to think out their ideas in terms of the
medium of embodiment and the object of ultimate perception unless they work mechanically and by rote. Probably
the esthetic quality of medieval cathedrals is due in
some measure to the fact that their constructions were
not so much controlled by plans and specifications
made in advance as is now the case. Plans grew as the
building grew. But even a Minerva-like product, if it
is artistic, presupposes a prior period of gestation
in which doings and perceptions projected in imagination
interact and mutually modify one another. Every work of
art follows the plan of, and pattern of, a complete
experience, rendering it more intensely and concentratedly
felt.

It is not so easy in the case of the perceiver and
appreciator to understand the intimate union of doing
and undergoing as it is in the case of the maker. We

are given to supposing that the former merely takes in what is there in finished form, instead of realizing that this taking in involves activities that are comparable to those of the creator. But receptivity is not passivity. It, too, is a process consisting of a series of responsive acts that accumulate toward objective fulfillment. Otherwise, there is not perception but recognition. The difference between the two is immense. Recognition is perception arrested before it has a chance to develop freely. In recognition there is a beginning of an act of perception. But this beginning is not allowed to serve the development of a full perception of the thing recognized. It is arrested at the point where it will serve some other purpose, as we recognize a man on the street in order to greet or to avoid him, not so as to see him for the sake of seeing what is there.

In recognition we fall back, as upon a stereotype, upon some previously formed scheme. Some detail or arrangement of details serves as cue for bare identification. It suffices in recognition to apply this bare outline as a stencil to the present object.

Sometimes in contact with a human being we are struck with
traits, perhaps of only physical characteristics, of which
we were not previously aware. We realize that we never
knew the person before; we had not seen him in any
pregnant sense. We now begin to study and to 'take in.'
Perception replaces bare recognition. There is an act of
reconstructive doing, and consciousness becomes fresh
and alive. This act of seeing involves the cooperation
of motor elements even though they remain implicit
and do not become overt, as well as cooperation of all
funded ideas that may serve to complete the new picture
that is forming. Recognition is too easy to arouse
vivid consciousness. There is not enough resistance
between new and old to secure consciousness of the
experience that is had. Even a dog that barks and
wags his tail joyously on seeing his master return is
more fully alive in his reception of his friend than is
a human being who is content with mere recognition.

Bare recognition is satisfied when a proper tag or
label is attached, 'proper' signifying one that serves a
purpose outside the act of recognition - as a salesman

168

identifies wares by a sample. It involves no stir of the organism, no inner commotion. But an act of perception proceeds by waves that extend serially throughout the entire organism. There is, therefore, no such thing in perception as seeing or hearing <u>plus</u> emotion. The perceived object or scene is emotionally pervaded throughout. When an aroused emotion does not permeate the material that is perceived or thought of, it is either preliminary or pathological.

The esthetic or undergoing phase of experience is receptive. It involves surrender. But adequate yielding of the self is possibly only through a controlled activity that may well be intense. In much of our intercourse with our surroundings we withdraw; sometimes from fear, if only of expending unduly our store of energy; sometimes from preoccupation with other matters, as in the case of recognition. Perception is an act of the going-out of energy in order to receive, not a withholding of energy. To steep ourselves in a subject-matter we have first to plunge into it. When we are only passive to a scene, it overwhelms us and, for lack of answering activity, we do

not perceive that which bears us down. We must summon
energy and pitch it at a responsive key in order to take
in.

Every one knows that it requires apprenticeship to
see through a microscope or telescope, and to see a landscape as the geologist sees it. The idea that esthetic
perception is an affair for odd moments is one reason
for the backwardness of the arts among us. The eye and
the visual apparatus may be intact; the object may be
physically there, the cathedral of Notre Dame, or Rembrandt's
portrait of Hendrik Stoeffel. In some bald sense,
the latter may be 'seen.' They may be looked at, possibly
recognized, and have their correct names attached. But
for lack of continuous interaction between the total
organism and the objects, they are not perceived, certainly
not esthetically. A crowd of visitors steered through a
picture-gallery by a guide, with attention called here
and there to some high point, does not perceive, only by
accident is there even interest in seeing a picture for
the sake of subject matter vividly realized.

For to perceive, a beholder must create his own

170

experience. And his creation must include relations comparable to those which the original producer underwent. They are not the same in any literal sense. But with the perceiver, as with the artist, there must be ordering of the elements of the whole that is in form, although not in details, the same as the process of organization the creator of the work consciously experienced. Without an act of recreation the object is not perceived as a work of art. The artist selected, simplified, clarified, abridged and condensed according to his interest. The beholder must go through these operations according to his point of view and interest. In both, an act of abstraction, that is of extraction of what is significant, takes place. In both, there is comprehension in its literal signification - that is, a gathering together of details and particulars physically scattered into an experienced whole. There is work done on the part of the percipient as there is on the part of the artist. The one who is too lazy, idle, or indurated in convention to perform this work will not see or hear. His 'appreciation' will be a mixture of scraps of learning with conformity

171

to norms of conventional admiration and with a confused,
even if genuine, emotional excitation.

The considerations that have been presented imply both
the community and the unlikeness, because of specific
emphasis, of an experience, in its pregnant sense, and
esthetic experience. The former has esthetic quality;
otherwise its materials would not be rounded out into a
single coherent experience. It is not possible to divide
In a vital experience the practical, emotional, and
intellectual from one another and to set the properties
of one over against the characteristics of the others.
The emotional phase binds parts together into a single
whole; 'intellectual' simply names the fact that the
experience has meaning; 'practical' indicates that the
organism is interacting with events and objects which
surround it. The most elaborate philosophic or scientific
inquiry and the most ambitious industrial or political
enterprise has, when its different ingredients constitute
an integral experience, esthetic quality. For then its
varied parts are linked to one another, and do not merely
succeed one another. And the parts through their experienced

172

linkage move toward a consummation and close, not merely to cessation in time. This consummation, moreover, does not wait in consciousness for the whole undertaking to be finished. It is anticipated throughout and is recurrently savored with special intensity.

Nevertheless, the experiences in question are dominantly intellectual or practical, rather than distinctively esthetic, because of the interest and purpose that initiate and control them. In an intellectual experience, the conclusion has value on its own account. It can be extracted as a formula or as a 'truth,' and can be used in its independent entirety as factor and guide in other inquiries. In a work of art there is no such single self-sufficient deposit. The end, the terminus, is significant not by itself but as the integration of the parts. It has no other existence. A drama or novel is not the final sentence, even if the characters are disposed of as living happily ever after. In a distinctively esthetic experience, characteristics that are subdued in other experiences are dominant; those that are subordinate are controlling - namely, the characteristics in virtue of which the experience is an integrated complete

173

experience on its own account.

In every integral experience there is form because
there is dynamic organization. I call the organization
dynamic because it takes time to complete it, because
it is a growth. There is inception, development, fulfillment.
Material is ingested and digested through interaction
with that vital organization of the results of prior
experience that constitutes the mind of the worker.
Incubation goes on until what is conceived is brought
forth and is rendered perceptible as part of the
common world. An esthetic experience can be crowded
into a moment only in the sense that a climax of prior
long enduring processes may arrive in an outstanding
movement which so sweeps everything else into it that
all else is forgotten. That which distinguishes an
experience as esthetic is conversion of resistance
and tensions, of excitations that in themselves are
temptations to diversion, into a movement toward an
inclusive and fulfilling close.

Experiencing like breathing is a rhythm of intakings
and outgivings. Their succession is punctuated and made

a rhythm by the existence of intervals, periods in which one phase is ceasing and the other is inchoate and pre- paring. William James aptly compared the course of a conscious experience to the alternate flights and perchings of a bird. The flights and perchings are intimately connected with one another; they are not so many unrelated lightings succeeded by a number of equally unrelated hoppings. Each resting place in experience is an undergoing in which is absorbed and taken home the consequences of prior doing, and, unless the doing is that of utter caprice or sheer routine, each doing carries in itself meaning that has been extracted and conserved. As with the advance of an army, all gains from what has been already effected are periodically consolidated, and always with a view to what is to be done next. If we move too rapidly, we get away from the base of supplies - of accrued meanings - and the experience is flustered, thin, and confused. If we dawdle too long after having extracted a net value, experience perishes of inanition.

The _form_ of the whole is therefore present in every member. Fulfilling, consummating, are continuous functions, not mere ends, located at one place only. An engraver, painter, or writer is in process of completing at every stage of his work. He must at each point retain and sum up what has gone before as a whole and with reference to a whole to come. Otherwise there is no consistency and no security in his successive acts. The series of doings in the rhythm of experience give variety and movement; they save the work from monotony and useless repetitions. The undergoings are the corresponding elements in the rhythm, and they supply unity; they save the work from the aimlessness of a mere succession of excitations. An object is peculiarly and dominantly esthetic, yielding the enjoyment characteristic of esthetic perception, when the factors that determine anything which can be called an experience are lifted high above the threshold of perception and are made manifest for their own sake."

AESTHETIC EXPERIENCE AS TRANSPARENCY

For a great many Westerners, Suzuki's name is synonymous
with Zen Buddhism itself. His remarks are included here in
order to furnish an Eastern perspective. A popular image
of the Oriental as a contemplator of nature is not without
some foundation; therefore, the present selection was chosen
so as to offer an account of the aesthetic experience of
nature rather than that of art. When Suzuki speaks of
" . . . the merging of subject and object in one absolute
Emptiness (sunyata)," he is suggesting that ultimate
reality is non-dual, empty of dichotomies rather than
asserting that absolute reality is a literal nothingness.
Such language seems to sharply contrast with the "psychical
distance" metaphor in Edward Bullough's treatment of
aesthetic experience.

For Suzuki, to have an aesthetic experience of nature
or to appreciate the manifold objects of nature requires
that one experience the metaphysical root from which all
things have issued forth. We are then told that the blending
of self with others is a requirement for an aesthetic grasp

of nature. Aesthetic experiences of nature, Suzuki concludes, always entail something religious. Where Bullough would tell us to insert psychical distance between ourselves and the aesthetic object, Suzuki urges us to throw our whole being into the activity of aesthetically experiencing nature. Finally, Suzuki warns us that if we suffer from confusions which grow out of any absolute bifurcation between subject and object, "our love of nature" will be polluted by such dualism. Trans chaotic, trans-practical, and trans-mundane elements are all discernible in Suzuki's statement.

THE AESTHETIC EXPERIENCE OF NATURE

"THE AESTHETIC aspect of Zen teaching is closely related
to Zen asceticism in that there is in both the absence
of selfhood and the merging of subject and object in one
absolute Emptiness (sunyata). This is a strange saying, but,
as the basic teaching of Zen, it is reiterated everywhere
in Zen literature. To explain this is a great philosophical
task, full of intellectual pitfalls. Not only does it require
arduous and sustained thinking, but frequently this very
thinking is apt to lead to grave misconceptions of the true
meaning of Zen experience. Therefore, as already hinted,
Zen avoids abstract statements and conceptual reasoning;
and its literature is almost nothing but endless citations
of the so-called 'anecdotes' or 'incidents' (innen in
Japanese) or 'questions and answers' (known as mondo).
To those who have not been initiated into its mystery, it
is a wild and unapproachable territory of briars and brambles.
The Zen masters, however, are not yielding; they insist on
having their own way of expressing themselves; they think
that in this respect they know best, and they are in the right

179

because the nature of their experience is determinative
as regards their method of communication or demonstration.
If I cite the following mondo to illustrate Zen aestheticism,
I hope you will not take me as purposely mystifying my
position.

While Rikko (Lu Keng), a high government official of
the T'ang dynasty, had a talk with his Zen master Nansen, [5]
the official quoted a saying of Sojo, [6] a noted monk-scholar
of an earlier dynasty:

> Heaven and earth and I are of the same root,
> The ten-thousand things and I are of one substance

and continued, 'Is not this a most remarkable statement?'

Nansen called the attention of the visitor to the
flowering plant in the garden and said, 'People of the
world look at these flowers as if they were in a dream.'

This 'story' or mondo eloquently describes the aesthetic
attitude of Zen toward objects of Nature. Most people do not

---

5 Nan-ch'uan (748-834). Hekigan-shu, case 40.
6 Seng-chao (384-414). Seng-chao, one of the four principal
   disciples of Kumarajiva (who came from Kucha, Central Asia,
   to Ch'ang-an, China, in 401), wrote several essays on Buddhism
   The quotation is from one of them. Its source is in the
   Chuang-tzu, II.

really know how to look at the flower; for one thing they stand away from it; they never grasp the spirit of it; as they have no firm hold of it, they are as if dreaming of a flower. The one who beholds is separated from the object which is beheld; there is an impassable gap between the two; and it is impossible for the beholder to come in touch inwardly with his object. Here is no grasping of actual facts as we face them. If heaven and earth, with all the manifold objects between them, issue from the one root which you and I also come from, this root must be firmly seized upon so that there is an actual experience of it; for it is in this experience that Nansen's flower in its natural beauty appealed to his aesthetic sense. The so-called Japanese love of Nature becomes related to Zen when we come to this experience of Nature appreciation, which is Nature-living.

Here we must remember that the experience of mere oneness is not enough for the real appreciation of Nature. This no doubt gives a philosophical foundation to the sentimentalism of the Nature-loving Japanese, who are thus helped to enter deeply into the secrets of their own

aesthetic consciousness. Sentimentalism to that extent is
purified, one may say. But the feeling of love is possible
in a world of multiplicity; Nansen's remark falls flat
where there is only sameness. It is true that people of the
world are dreaming, because they do not see into the real
foundation of existence. The balancing of unity and multiplicity or, better, the merging of self with others as in
the philosophy of the Avatamsaka (Kegon) is absolutely
necessary to the aesthetic understanding of Nature.

Tennyson says:

> Little flower - but if I could understand
> What you are, root and all, and all in all,
> I should know what God and man is.

The beauty of the little flower in the crannied wall is
really appreciated only when it is referred to the ultimate
reason of all things. But it goes without saying that this
is not to be done in a merely philosophical and conceptual
way, but in the way Zen proposes to accomplish it: not in a
Pantheistic way, nor in a quietistic way, but in the 'living'
way as has been done by Nansen and his followers. To do this
and to appreciate Nansen truly, one must first greet Rikko
and be friendly with him; for it is in this way that one can

182

feel the force of the remark made by Nansen. The genuine beauty of the flower as he saw it is for the first time reflected in one's soul-mirror.

The aesthetic appreciation of Nature always involves something religious. And by being 'religious' I mean being 'superworldly,' going beyond the world of relativity, where we are bound to encounter oppositions and limitations. The oppositions and limitations which confront every movement of ours, physical and psychological, put a stop, also, to the free flow of our aesthetical feeling toward its objects. Beauty is felt when there is freedom of motion and freedom of expression. Beauty is not in form but in the meaning it expresses, and this meaning is felt when the observing subject throws his whole being into the bearer of the meaning and moves along with it. This is possible only when he lives in a 'superworld' where no mutually excluding oppositions take place, or rather when the mutually excluding oppositions of which we are always too conscious in this world of multiplicities are taken up even as they are into something of a higher order than they. Aestheticism now merges into religion.

Sir George Sansom makes this comment concerning the Zen love of Nature (Japan, A Short Cultural History, p. 392): 'But the Zen artists and the Zen poets - and it is often hard to say where their poetry ends and their painting begins - feel no antithesis between man and Nature, and are conscious even of an identity rather than a kinship. What interests them is not the restless movement on the surface of life, but (as Professor Anezaki puts it) the eternal tranquillity seen through and behind change.' This is not Zen at all. Both Professor Anezaki and Sir George Sansom fail to grasp the true Zen attitude toward Nature. It is not an experience of identification, nor is it the feeling of 'eternal tranquillity' they dream of. If the poets and the artists linger with that which is felt 'through and behind change,' they are still walking hand in hand with Rikko and Sojo, they are far, far from being friends of Nansen. The real flower is enjoyed only when the poet-artist lives with it, in it; and when even a sense of identity is no longer here, much less the 'eternal tranquillity.'

Thus I wish to emphasize that Zen does not see any

184

such thing as is designated 'the restless movement on the surface of life.' For life is one integral and indivisible whole, with neither surface nor interior; hence no 'restless movement' which can be separated from life itself. As was explained in the case of Ummon's 'golden-haired lion,' life moves in its complete oneness, whether restlessly or serenely, as you may conceive it; your interpretation does not alter the fact. Zen takes hold of life in its wholeness and moves 'restlessly' with it or stays quietly with it. Wherever there is any sign of life at all, there is Zen. When, however, the 'eternal tranquillity' is abstracted from 'the restless movement on the surface of life,' it sinks into death, and there is no more of its 'surface' either. The tranquillity of Zen is in the midst of 'the boiling oil,' the surging waves, and in the flames enveloping the god Acala.

Kanzan (Han-shan) was one of the most famous poet-lunatics of the T'ang dynasty - Zen often produces such 'lunatics' - and one of his poems reads:

> My mind is like the autumnal moon;
> And how clear and transparent the deep pool!
> No comparison, however, in any form is possible,
> It is altogether beyond description.

Superficially, this poem may suggest the idea of
tranquillity or serenity. The autumnal moon is serene,
and its light uniformly pervading the fields and rivers
and mountains may make us think of the oneness of things.
But this is where Kanzan hesitates to draw any comparison
between his feelings and things of this world. The
reason is sure to take the pointing finger for the moon,
as our worthy critics frequently do. To tell the truth,
there is here not the remotest hint of tranquillity or
serenity, nor of the identity of Nature and man. If
anything is suggested here, it is the idea of utmost
transparency which the poet feels through and through.
He is entirely lifted out of his bodily existence,
including both his objective world and his subjective
mind. He has no such interfering mediums inside and
outside. He is thoroughly pure, and from this position
of absolute purity or transparency he looks out on a
world of multiplicity so called. He sees flowers and
mountains and ten thousand other things, and will pro-

186

nounce them beautiful and satisfying. 'The restless movements' are appreciated just as much as 'the eternal tranquillity.' It goes entirely against the spirit of Zen and the Japanese idea of love of Nature to imagine that the Japanese Zen poets and artists avoid the restlessness of a world of multiplicity in order to get into the eternal tranquillity of abstract ideas. Let us first get an experience of transparency, and we are able to love Nature and its multifarious objects, though not dualistically. As long as we harbor conceptual illusions arising from the separation of subject and object and believe them final, the transparency is obscured, and our love of Nature is contaminated with dualism and sophistry.

To quote another poet of Zen, this time a Japanese and the founder of a great Zen monastery called Eigenji in the province of Omi - his name is Jakushitsu (1290-1367):

The wind stirs the flying waterfall and sends in refreshing music;
The moon is risen over the opposite peak and the bamboo shadows are cast over my paper window:
As I grow older, the mountain retreat appeals all the more strongly to my feeling;
Even when I am buried, after death, underneath the rock, my bones will be as thoroughly transparent as ever.

187

Some readers may be tempted to read into this poem
a sense of solitude or quietness, but that this altogether
misses the point is apparent to those who know at all
what Zen is. Unless the Zen artist is saturated with the
feeling Jakushitsu graphically expresses here, he cannot
expect to understand Nature, nor can he truly love Nature.
Transparency is the keynote to the Zen understanding of
Nature, and it is from this that its love of Nature starts.
When people say that Zen has given a philosophical and
religious foundation to the Japanese love of Nature,
this Zen attitude or feeling must be taken fully into
consideration. When Sir George Sansom surmises that
'they aristocrats, monks, and artists were moved by a
belief that all nature is permeated by one spirit,'
and that 'it was the aim of the Zen practitioner in
particular, by purging his mind of egotistic commotions,
to reach a tranquil, intuitive realization of his
identity with the universe' (p. 392), he ignores the
part Zen has really contributed to the Japanese aesthetic
appreciation of Nature. He cannot shake off the idea of
'eternal tranquillity' or of a spiritual identity between

subject and object.

The idea of 'spiritual identity' by which our egotistic commotions are kept quiet and in which eternal tranquillity is experienced is an alluring idea. Most students of Oriental culture and philosophy grasp at it as giving them the key to the inscrutable psychology of the Eastern peoples. But this is the Western mind trying to solve the mystery in its own way - in fact, it cannot do anything else. As far as we Japanese are concerned, we are unable to accept without comment this interpretation offered by the Western critics. Plainly speaking, Zen does not acknowledge 'one spirit' permeating all Nature, nor does it attempt to realize identity by purging its mind of 'egotistic commotions. According to the author of this statement, the grasping of 'one spirit' is evidently the realization of identity that is left behind when the purgation of egotism is effected. While it is difficult to refute this idea convincingly as long as we are arguing along the logical line of Yes and No, I will try to make my point clearer in the following paragraphs."

AESTHETIC EXPERIENCE AS UNIQUE EMOTION

For Clive Bell, "significant form" is the defining characteristic of art. Developing this conception of art, he argues that aesthetic experience is a matter of responding to significant form. One must react exclusively to formal components (line, color, shape, and composition) if he is to have an aesthetic experience. All representational elements are regarded as irrelevant; in fact, they can have the harmful effect of misdirecting one's attention away from the crucial structural properties which constitute art. Simply stated, subject matter as such does not matter. Bell's point seems to be that one who concentrates upon the formal aspects in an art work will find himself in a world with a significance all its own; this significance is unrelated to the significance of life; it is a world of unique emotion. Referential features must be apprehended non-referentially as pure forms devoid of their usual associations if one is to have the peculiar emotion which distinguishes the aesthetic experience.

Historically, Bell's value lies in drawing attention to

191

the structural ingredients in art works; previous thinkers had emphasized the representational or emotive aspects of art. At the same time, Bell helped open the door for the entrance of much contemporary art, for his theory offered an approach to non-representational art. Bell himself held that his theory was especially rich, because it could be applied to all ages and cultures. On the negative side, Bell's request that one focus entirely upon form can be criticized as unrealistic, for it can be argued that it is not possible to wholly abstract associations with life from one's encounter with an art work. Moreover, even if it were possible to perform such an abstraction, it might be seen as undesirable. Consider the powerful interplay of form and content in Picasso's painting "Guernica" which discourages one from trying to separate the formal energy from the indignation which it seeks to express. Again, Bell's concentration upon form can hardly do justice to literary art. Bell's claim that there is a peculiar aesthetic emotion can be criticized by those who insist upon recognizing a continuity rather than an absolute dichotomy between art and life. Perhaps

192

what Bell calls a unique aesthetic emotion is simply a more or less intense form of some life emotion or other. Introspection seems to be as good a guide as any in considering such issues. To many readers, Bell will remain a figure who carried the trans-pragmatic and trans-mundane aspects of aesthetic experience to unacceptable conclusions.

THE AESTHETIC HYPOTHESIS

"IT IS improbable that more nonsense has been written about
aesthetics than about anything else: the literature of the
subject is not large enough for that. It is certain, however, that about no subject with which I am acquainted has
so little been said that is at all to the purpose. The
explanation is discoverable. He who would elaborate a
plausible theory of aesthetics must possess two qualities -
artistic sensibility and a turn for clear thinking. Without
sensibility a man can have no aesthetic experience, and,
obviously, theories not based on broad and deep aesthetic
experience are worthless. Only those for whom art is a
constant source of passionate emotion can possess the data
from which profitable theories may be deduced; but to
deduce profitable theories even from accurate data involves
a certain amount of brain-work, and, unfortunately, robust
intellects and delicate sensibilities are not inseparable.
As often as not, the hardest thinkers have had no aesthetic
experience whatever. I have a friend blessed with an intellect
as keen as a drill, who, though he takes an interest in

195

aesthetics, has never during a life of almost forty years been guilty of an aesthetic emotion. So, having no faculty for distinguishing a work of art from a handsaw, he is apt to rear up a pyramid of irrefragable argument on the hypothesis that a handsaw is a work of art. This defect robs his perspicuous and subtle reasoning of much of its value; for it has ever been a maxim that faultless logic can win but little credit for conclusions that are based on premises notoriously false. Every cloud, however, has its silver lining, and this insensibility, though unlucky in that it makes my friend incapable of choosing a sound basis for his argument, mercifully blinds him to the absurdity of his conclusions while leaving him in full enjoyment of his masterly dialectic. People who set out from the hypothesis that Sir Edwin Landseer was the finest painter that ever lived will feel no uneasiness about an aesthetic which proves that Giotto was the worst. So, my friend, when he arrives very logically at the conclusion that a work of art should be small or round or smooth, or that to appreciate fully a picture you should pace smartly before it or set it spinning like a top,

196

cannot guess why I ask him whether he has lately been to Cambridge, a place he sometimes visits.

On the other hand, people who respond immediately and surely to works of art, though, in my judgment, more enviable than men of massive intellect but slight sensibility, are often quite as incapable of talking sense about aesthetics. Their heads are not always very clear. They possess the data on which any system must be based; but, generally, they want the power that draws correct inferences from true data. Having received aesthetic emotions from works of art, they are in a position to seek out the quality common to all that have moved them, but, in fact, they do nothing of the sort. I do not blame them. Why should they bother to examine feelings when for them to feel is enough? Why should they stop to think when they are not very good at thinking? Why should they hunt for a common quality in all objects that move them in a particular way when they can linger over the many delicious and peculiar charms of each as it comes? So, if they write criticism and call it aesthetics, if they imagine that they are talking about Art when they are talking about particular works of art or

197

even about the technique of painting, if loving particular works they find tedious the consideration of art in general, perhaps they have chosen the better part. If they are not curious about the nature of their emotion, nor about the qualit common to all objects that provoke it, they have my sympathy, and, as what they say is often charming and suggestive, my admiration too. Only let no one suppose that what they write and talk is aesthetics; it is criticism, or just 'shop.' The starting point for all systems of aesthetics must be the personal experience of a peculiar emotion. The objects that provoke this emotion we call works of art. All sensitive people agree that there is a peculiar emotion provoked by works of art. I do not mean, of course, that all works provoke the same emotion. On the contrary, every work produces a different emotion. But all these emotions are recognisably the same in kind; so far, at any rate, the best opinion is on my side. That there is a particular kind of emotion provoked by works of visual art, and that this emotion is provoked by every kind of visual art, by pictures, sculptures, buildings, pots, carvings, textiles, etc., etc., is not disputed, I think, by anyone capable of feeling it. This emotion is called the aesthetic emotion; and if we can discover some quality common and peculiar to all the objects that provoke it, we shall have solved what I take to be the central problem of aesthetics. We shall have discovered the essential quality in a work of art, the quality that distinguishes works of art from all other classes of objects.

For either all works of visual art have some common quality, or when we speak of 'works of art' we gibber. Everyone speaks of 'art,' making a mental classification by which he distinguishes the class 'works of art' from all other classes. What is the justification of this classification? What is the quality common and peculiar to all members of this class? Whatever it be, no doubt it is often found in company with other qualities; but they are adventitious - it is essential. There must be some one quality without which a work of art cannot exist; possessing which, in the least degree, no work is altogether worthless. What is this quality? What quality is shared by all objects that provoke our aesthetic emotions? What quality is common to Sta. Sophia and the windows at Chartres, Mexican sculpture, a Persian bowl, Chinese carpets, Giotto's frescoes at Padua, and the masterpieces of Poussin, Piero della Francesca, and Cezanne? Only one answer seems possible - significant form. In each, lines and colours combined in a particular way, certain forms and relations of forms, stir our aesthetic emotions. These relations and combinations of lines and colours, these aesthetically moving forms, I call 'Significant Form'; and 'Significant Form' is the one quality common to all works of visual art.

At this point it may be objected that I am making aesthetic a purely subjective business, since my only data are personal experiences of a particular emotion. It will be said that the objects that provoke this emotion vary with each individual, and that therefore a system of aesthetics can have no objective validity. It must be replied that any system of aesthetics which pretends to be based on some objective truth is so palpably ridiculous as not to be worth discussing. We have no other means of recognising a work of art than our feeling for it. The objects that provoke aesthetic emotion vary with each individual. Aesthetic judgments are, as the saying goes, matters of taste; and about tastes, as everyone

200

is proud to admit, there is no disputing. A good critic may be able to make me see in a picture that had left me cold things that I had overlooked, till at last, receiving the aesthetic emotion, I recognise it as a work of art. To be continually pointing out those parts, the sum, or rather the combination, of which unite to produce significant form, is the function of criticism. But it is useless for a critic to tell me that something is a work of art; he must make me feel it for myself. This he can do only by making me see; he must get at my emotions through my eyes. Unless he can make me see something that moves me, he cannot force my emotions. I have no right to consider anything a work of art to which I cannot react emotionally; and I have no right to look for the essential quality in anything that I have not felt to be a work of art. The critic can affect my aesthetic theories only by affecting my aesthetic experience. All systems of aesthetics must be based on personal experience - that is to say, they must be subjective.

Yet, though all aesthetic theories must be based on

aesthetic judgments, and ultimately all aesthetic judgments must be matters of personal taste, it would be rash to assert that no theory of aesthetics can have general validity. For, though A, B, C, D are the works that move me, and A, D, E, F the works that move you, it may well be that x is the only quality believed by either of us to be common to all the works in his list. We may all agree about aesthetics, and yet differ about particular works of art. We may differ as to the presence or absence of the quality x. My immediate object will be to show that significant form is the only quality common and peculiar to all the works of visual art that move me; and I will ask those whose aesthetic experience does not tally with mine to see whether this quality is not also, in their judgment, common to all works that move them, and whether they can discover any other quality of which the same can be said.

Also at this point a query arises, irrelevant indeed, but hardly to be suppressed: 'Why are we so profoundly moved by forms related in a particular way?' The question is extremely interesting, but irrelevant to aesthetics. In pure aesthetics we have only to consider our emotion and its object: for the

purposes of aesthetics we have no right, neither is there
any necessity, to pry behind the object into the state of
mind of him who made it. Later, I shall attempt to answer
the question; for by so doing I may be able to develop
my theory of the relation of art to life. I shall not,
however, be under the delusion that I am rounding off my
theory of aesthetics. For a discussion of aesthetics, it
need be agreed only that forms arranged and combined
according to certain unknown and mysterious laws do move
us in a particular way, and that it is the business of
an artist so to combine and arrange them that they shall
move us. These moving combinations and arrangements I
have called, for the sake of convenience and for a reason
that will appear later, 'Significant Form.'

A third interruption has to be met.

'Are you forgetting about colour?' someone inquires.
Certainly not; my term 'significant form' included combinations of lines and of colours. The distinction between
form and colour is an unreal one; you cannot conceive a
colourless line or a colourless space; neither can you
conceive a formless relation of colours. In a black and white

drawing the spaces are all white and all are bounded by black lines; you cannot imagine a boundary line without any content, or content without a boundary line. Therefore, when I speak of significant form, I mean a combination of lines and colours (counting white and black as colours) that moves me aesthetically.

Some people may be surprised at my not having called this 'beauty.' Of course, to those who define beauty as 'combinations of lines and colours that provoke aesthetic emotion,' I willingly concede the right of substituting their word for mine. But most of us, however strict we may be, are apt to apply the epithet 'beautiful' to objects that do not provoke that peculiar emotion produced by works of art. Everyone, I suspect, has called a butterfly or a flower beautiful. Does anyone feel the same kind of emotion for a butterfly or a flower that he feels for a cathedral or a picture? Surely, it is not what I call an aesthetic emotion that most of us feel, generally, for natural beauty. I shall suggest, later, that some people may, occasionally, see in nature what we see in art, and feel for her an aesthetic emotion; but I am

204

satisfied that, as a rule, most people feel a very different kind of emotion for birds and flowers and the wings of butterflies from that which they feel for pictures, pots, temples and statues. Why these beautiful things do not move us as works of art move is another, and not an aesthetic, question. For our immediate purpose we have to discover only what quality is common to objects that do move us as works of art. In the last part of this chapter, when I try to answer the question - 'Why are we so profoundly moved by some combinations of lines and colours?' I shall hope to offer an acceptable explanation of why we are less profoundly moved by others.

Since we call a quality that does not raise the characteristic aesthetic emotion 'Beauty,' it would be misleading to call by the same name the quality that does. To make 'beauty' the object of the aesthetic emotion, we must give to the world an over-strict and unfamiliar definition. Everyone sometimes uses 'beauty' in an unaesthetic sense; most people habitually do so. To everyone, except perhaps here and there an occasional aesthete, the commonest sense of the word is unaesthetic. Of its grosser abuse, patent in our chatter about 'beautiful huntin'' and 'beautiful shootin',' I need not take account; it would be open to the precious to reply that they never do so abuse it. Besides, here there is no danger of confusion between the aesthetic and the non-aesthetic use; but when we speak of a beautiful woman there is. When an ordinary man speaks of a beautiful woman he certainly does not mean only that she moves him aesthetically; but when an artist calls a withered old hag beautiful he may sometimes mean what he means when he calls a battered torso beautiful. The ordinary man, if he be also a man of taste, will call the battered torso beautiful, but he will not call a withered hag beautiful because, in the matter of women, it is not to the aesthetic quality that the hag may possess, but to some other quality that he assigns the epithet. Indeed, most of us never dream of going for aesthetic emotions to human beings, from whom we ask something very different. This 'something,' when we find it in a young woman, we are apt to call 'beauty.' We live in a nice age. With the man-in-the-street 'beautiful' is more often than not synonymous with 'desirable'; the word does not necessarily connote any aesthetic reaction whatever,

206

and I am tempted to believe that in the minds of many the
sexual flavour of the word is stronger than the aesthetic.
I have noticed a consistency in those to whom the most
beautiful thing in the world is a beautiful woman,
and the next most beautiful thing a picture of one.
The confusion between aesthetic and sensual beauty is not
in their case so great as might be supposed. Perhaps
there is none; for perhaps they have never had an aesthetic
emotion to confuse with their other emotions. The art
that they call 'beautiful' is generally closely related
to the women. A beautiful picture is a photograph of a
pretty girl; beautiful music, the music that provokes
emotions similar to those provoked by young ladies in
musical farces; and beautiful poetry, the poetry that
recalls the same emotions felt, twenty years earlier,
for the rector's daughter. Clearly the word 'beauty'
is used to connote the objects of quite distinguishable
emotions, and that is a reason for not employing a term
which would land me inevitably in confusions and mis-
understandings with my readers.

On the other hand, with those who judge it more exact

207

to call these combinations and arrangements of form that
provoke our aesthetic emotions, not 'significant form,'
but 'significant relations of form,' and then try to
make the best of two worlds, the aesthetic and the
metaphysical, by calling these relations 'rhythm,' I
have no quarrel whatever. Having made it clear that
by 'significant form' I mean arrangements and combinations that move us in a particular way, I willingly
join hands with those who prefer to give a different name
to the same thing.

The hypothesis that significant form is the essential
quality in a work of art has at least one merit denied to
many more famous and more striking - it does help to
explain things. We are all familiar with pictures that
interest us and excite our admiration, but do not move
us as works of art. To this class belongs what I call
'Descriptive Painting' - that is, painting in which forms
are used not as objects of emotion, but as means of
suggesting emotion or conveying information. Portraits
of psychological and historical value, topographical
works, pictures that tell stories and suggest situations,

208

illustrations of all sorts, belong to this class. That
we all recognize the distinction is clear, for who has
not said that such and such a drawing was excellent as
illustration, but as a work of art worthless? Of course
many descriptive pictures possess, amongst other qualities,
formal significance, and are therefore works of art:
but many more do not. They interest us; they may move us
too in a hundred different ways, but they do not move us
aesthetically. According to my hypothesis they are not
works of art. They leave untouched our aesthetic emotions
because it is not their forms but the ideas or information
suggested or conveyed by their forms that affect us.

Few pictures are better known or liked than Frith's
'Paddington Station'; certainly I should be the last to
grudge it its popularity. Many a weary forty minutes have
I whiled away disentangling its fascinating incidents and
forging for each an imaginary past and an improbable future.
But certain though it is that Frith's masterpiece, or
engravings of it, have provided thousands with half-hours
of curious and fanciful pleasure, it is not less certain
that no one has experienced before it one half-second of

aesthetic rapture - and this although the picture contains several pretty passages of colour, and is by no means badly painted. 'Paddington Station' is not a work of art; it is an interesting and amusing document. In it line and colour are used to recount anecdotes, suggest ideas, and indicate the manners and customs of an age: they are not used to provoke aesthetic emotion. Forms and the relations of forms were for Frith not objects of emotion, but means of suggesting emotion and conveying ideas.

The ideas and information conveyed by 'Paddington Station' are so amusing and so well presented that the picture has considerable value and is well worth preserving. But, with the perfection of photographic processes and of the cinematograph, pictures of this sort are becoming otiose. Who doubts that one of those Daily Mirror photographers in collaboration with a Daily Mail reporter can tell us far more about 'London day by day' than any Royal Academician? For an account of manners and fashions we shall go, in future, to photographs, supported by a little bright journalism, rather than to descriptive painting. Had the imperial academicians of Nero, instead of manufacturing incredibly loathsome imitations of the antique, recorded in fresco and mosaic the manners and fashions of their day, their stuff, though artistic rubbish, would now be an historical gold-mine. If only they had been Friths instead of being Alma Tademas! But photography has made impossible any such transmutation of modern rubbish. Therefore it must be confessed that pictures in the Frith tradition are grown superfluous; they merely waste the hours of able men who might be more profitably employed in works of a wider beneficence. Still, they are not unpleasant, which is more than can be said for that kind of descriptive painting of which 'The Doctor' is the most flagrant example. Of course 'The Doctor' is not a work of art. In it form is not used as an object of emotion, but as a means of suggesting emotions. This alone suffers to make it nugatory; it is worse than nugatory because the emotion it suggests is false. What it suggests is not pity and admiration but a sense of complacency in our own pitifulness and generosity. It is sentimental. Art is above morals, or, rather, all art is moral because, as I hope to show presently, works

211

of art are immediate means to good. Once we have judged
a thing a work of art, we have judged it ethically of the
first importance and put it beyond the reach of the
moralist. But descriptive pictures which are not works
of art, and, therefore, are not necessarily means to
good states of mind, are proper objects of the ethical
philosopher's attention. Not being a work of art,
'The Doctor' has none of the immense ethical value
possessed by all objects that provoke aesthetic ecstasy;
and the state of mind to which it is a means, as illustration, appears to me undesirable.

The works of those enterprising young men, the
Italian Futurists, are notable examples of descriptive
painting. Like the Royal Academicians, they use form,
not to provoke aesthetic emotions, but to convey information and ideas. Indeed, the published theories of the
Futurists prove that their pictures ought to have nothing
whatever to do with art. Their social and political
theories are respectable, but I would suggest to young
Italian painters that it is possible to become a Futurist
in thought and action and yet remain an artist, if one

has the luck to be born one. To associate art with politics is always a mistake. Futurist pictures are descriptive because they aim at presenting in line and colour the chaos of the mind at a particular moment; their forms are not intended to promote aesthetic emotion but to convey information. These forms, by the way, whatever may be the nature of the ideas they suggest, are themselves anything but revolutionary. In such Futurist pictures as I have seen - perhaps I should except some by Severini - the drawing, whenever it becomes representative as it frequently does, is found to be in that soft and common convention brought into fashion by Besnard some thirty years ago, and much affected by Beaux-Art students ever since. As works of art, the Futurist pictures are negligible; but they are not to be judged as works of art. A good Futurist picture would succeed as a good piece of psychology succeeds; it would reveal, through line and colour, the complexities of an interesting state of mind. If Futurist pictures seem to fail, we must seek an explanation, not in a lack of artistic qualities that they never were intended to possess, but rather in the minds the states

213

of which they are intended to reveal.

Most people who care much about art find that of the
work that moves them most the greater part is what scholars
call 'Primitive.' Of course there are bad primitives.
For instance, I remember going, full of enthusiasm, to see
one of the earliest Romanesque churches in Poitiers
(Notre-Dame-la-Grande), and finding it as ill-proportioned,
over-decorated, coarse, fat and heavy as any better class
building by one of those highly civilised architects who
flourished a thousand years earlier or eight hundred later.
But such exceptions are rare. As a rule primitive art is
good - and here again my hypothesis is helpful - for, as a
rule, it is also free from descriptive qualities. In
primitive art you will find no accurate representation;
you will find only significant form. Yet no other art
moves us so profoundly. Whether we consider Sumerian
sculpture or pre-dynastic Egyptian art, or archaic Greek,
or the Wei and T'ang masterpieces, [1] or those early Japanese

---

1 The existence of the Ku K'ai-chih makes it clear that the
  art of this period (fifth to eighth centuries), was a typical
  primitive movement. To call the great vital art of the Liang,

Chen, Wei, and Tang dynasties a development out of the
exquisitely refined and exhausted art of the Han decadence -
from which Ku K'ai-chih is a delicate straggler - is to call
Romanesque sculpture a development out of Praxiteles.
Between the two something has happened to refill the
stream of art. What had happened in China was the spiritual
and emotional revolution that followed the onset of Buddhism.

works of which I had the luck to see a few superb examples

(especially two wooden Bodhisattvas) at the Shepherd's

Bush Exhibition in 1910, or whether, coming nearer home,

we consider the primitive Byzantine art of the sixth century

and its primitive developments amongst the Western

barbarians, or, turning far afield, we consider that

mysterious and majestic art that flourished in Central

and South America before the coming of the white men,

in every case we observe three common characteristics -

absence of representation, absence of technical swagger,

sublimely impressive form. Nor is it hard to discover

the connection between these three. Formal significance

loses itself in preoccupation with exact representation

and ostentatious cunning. [1]

_____

[1] This is not to say that exact representation is bad
in itself. It is indifferent. A perfectly represented
form may be significant, only it is fatal to sacrifice

215

significance to representation. The quarrel between
significance and illusion seems to be as old as art itself,
and I have little doubt that what makes most palaeolithic
art so bad is a preoccupation with exact representation.
Evidently palaeolithic draughtsmen had no sense of the
significance of form. Their art resembles that of the
more capable and sincere Royal Academicians: it is a
little higher than that of Sir Edward Poynter and a little
lower than that of the late Lord Leighton. That this is no
paradox let the cave-drawings of Altamira, or such works
as the sketches of horses found at Bruniquel and now in
the British Museum, bear witness. If the ivory head of
a girl from the Grotte du Pape, Brassempouy (Musee St. Germain)
and the ivory torso found at the same place (Collection
St. Cric), be, indeed, palaeolithic, then there were
good palaeolithic artists who created and did not imitate
form. Neolithic art is, of course, a very different matter.

Naturally, it is said that if there is little represen-

tation and less saltimbancery in primitive art, that is

because the primitives were unable to catch a likeness or

cut intellectual capers. The contention is beside the

point. There is truth in it, no doubt, though, were I a

critic whose reputation depended on a power of impressing

the public with a semblance of knowledge, I should be more

cautious about urging it than such people generally are.

For to suppose that the Byzantine masters wanted skill, or

could not have created an illusion had they wished to do so,

seems to imply ignorance of the amazingly dexterous realism

of the notoriously bad works of that age. Very often, I fear,

the misrepresentation of the primitives must be attributed
to what the critics call, 'wilful distortion.' Be that as
it may, the point is that, either from want of skill or
want of will, primitive neither create illusions, not
make display of extravagant accomplishment, but concentrate
their energies on the one thing needful - the creation of
form. Thus have they created the finest works of art that
we possess.

Let no one imagine that representation is bad in itself;
a realistic form may be as significant, in its place as part
of the design, as an abstract. But if a representative form
has value, it is as form, not as representation. The representative element in a work of art may or may not be harmful;
always it is irrelevant. For, to appreciate a work of art
we need bring with us nothing from life, no knowledge of
its ideas and affairs, no familiarity with its emotions.
Art transports us from the world of man's activity to a world
of aesthetic exaltation. For a moment we are shut off from
human interests; our anticipation and memories are arrested;
we are lifted above the stream of life. The pure mathematician
rapt in his studies knows a state of mind which I take to be

similar, if not identical. He feels an emotion for his
speculations which arises from no perceived relation
between them and the lives of men, but springs, inhuman
or super-human, from the heart of an abstract science.
I wonder, sometimes, whether the appreciators of art and
of mathematical solutions are not even more closely
allied. Before we feel an aesthetic emotion for a combination of forms, do we not perceive intellectually the
rightness and necessity of the combination? If we do,
it would explain the fact that passing rapidly through
a room we recognise a picture to be good, although we
cannot say that it has provoked much emotion. We seem
to have recognised intellectually the rightness of its
forms without staying to fix our attention, and collect,
as it were, their emotional significance. If this were so,
it would be permissible to inquire whether it was the forms
themselves or our perception of their rightness and necessity
that caused aesthetic emotion. But I do not think I need
linger to discuss the matter here. I have been inquiring
why certain combinations of forms move us; I should not
have travelled by other roads had I enquired, instead,

why certain combinations are perceived to be right and
necessary, and why our perception of their rightness and
necessity is moving. What I have to say is this: the
rapt philosopher, and he who contemplates a work of art,
inhabit a world with an intense and peculiar significance
of its own; that significance is unrelated to the
significance of life. In this world the emotions of
life find no place. It is a world with emotions of its
own.

To appreciate a work of art we need bring with us
nothing but a sense of form and colour and a knowledge
of three-dimensional space. That bit of knowledge, I
admit, is essential to the appreciation of many great
works, since many of the most moving forms ever created
are in three dimensions. To see a cube or a rhomboid as
a flat pattern is to lower its significance, and a
sense of three-dimensional space is essential to the
full appreciation of most architectural forms. Pictures
which would be insignificant if we saw them as flat
patterns are profoundly moving because, in fact, we see
them as related planes. If the representation of three-

dimensional space is to be called 'representation,'
then I agree that there is one kind of representation which
is not irrelevant. Also, I agree that along with our
feeling for line and colour we must bring with us our
knowledge of space if we are to make the most of every
kind of form. Nevertheless, there are magnificent
designs to an appreciation of which this knowledge
is not necessary: so, though it is not irrelevant to the
appreciation of some works of art it is not essential to
the appreciation of all. What we must say is that the
representation of three-dimensional space is neither
irrelevant nor essential to all art, and that every other
sort of representation is irrelevant.

That there is an irrelevant representative or descriptive element in many great works of art is not in the
least surprising. Why it is not surprising I shall try to
show elsewhere. Representation is not of necessity baneful,
and highly realistic forms may be extremely significant.
Very often, however, representation is a sign of weakness in
an artist. A painter too feeble to create forms that
provoke more than a little aesthetic emotion will try to eke

that little out by suggesting the emotions of life. To evoke the emotions of life he must use representation. Thus a man will paint an execution, and, fearing to miss with his first barrel of significant form, will try to hit with his second by raising an emotion of fear or pity. But if in the artist an inclination to play upon the emotions of life is often the sign of a flickering inspiration, in the spectator a tendency to seek, behind form, the emotions of life is a sign of defective sensibility always. It means that his aesthetic emotions are weak or, at any rate, imperfect. Before a work of art people who feel little or no emotion for pure form find themselves at a loss. They are deaf men at a concert. They know that they are in the presence of something great, but they lack the power of apprehending it. They know that they ought to feel for it a tremendous emotion, but it happens that the particular kind of emotion it can raise is one that they can feel hardly or not at all. And so they read into the forms of the work those facts and ideas for which they are capable of feeling emotion, and feel for them the emotions that they can feel - the ordinary emotions of life.

221

When confronted by a picture instinctively they refer
back its forms to the world from which they came. They
treat created form as though it were imitated form,
a picture as though it were a photograph. Instead of going
out on the stream of art into a new world of aesthetic
experience, they turn a sharp corner and come straight home
to the world of human interests. For them the significance
of a work of art depends on what they bring to it; no
new thing is added to their lives, only the old material is
stirred. A good work of visual art carries a person who
is capable of appreciating it out of life into ecstasy: to
use art as a means to the emotions of life is to use a
telescope for reading the news. You will notice that
people who cannot feel pure aesthetic emotions remember
pictures by their subjects; whereas people who can, as
often as not, have no idea what the subject of a picture is.
They have never noticed the representative element, and so
when they discuss pictures they talk about the shapes of
forms and the relations and quantities of colours. Often
they can tell by the quality of a single line whether or
no a man is a good artist. They are concerned only with

lines and colours, their relations and quantities and qualities; but from these they win an emotion more profound and far more sublime than any that can be given by the description of facts and ideas.

This last sentence has a very confident ring - over-confident, some may think. Perhaps I shall be able to justify it, and make my meaning clearer too, if I give an account of my own feelings about music. I am not really musical. I do not understand music well. I find musical form exceedingly difficult to apprehend, and I am sure that the profounder subtleties of harmony and rhythm more often than not escape me. The form of a musical composition must be simple indeed if I am to grasp it honestly. My opinion about music is not worth having. Yet, sometimes, at a concert, though my appreciation of the music is limited and humble, it is pure. Sometimes, though I have a poor understanding, I have a clean palate. Consequently, when I am feeling bright and clear and intent, at the beginning of a concert for instance, when something that I can grasp is being played, I get from music that pure aesthetic emotion that I get from visual art. It is less

intense, and the rapture is evanescent; I understand music
too ill for music to transport me far into the world of pure
aesthetic ecstasy. But at moments I do appreciate music
as pure musical form, as sounds combined according to the
laws of a mysterious necessity, as pure art with a tremendous
significance of its own and no relation whatever to the
significance of life; and in those moments I lose myself
in that infinitely sublime state of mind to which pure
visual form transports me. How inferior is my normal state
of mind at a concert. Tired or perplexed, I let slip my
sense of form, my aesthetic emotion collapses, and I begin
weaving into the harmonies, that I cannot grasp, the ideas
of life. Incapable of feeling the austere emotions of art,
I begin to read into the musical forms human emotions of
terror and mystery, love and hate, and spend the minutes,
pleasantly enough, in a world of turbid and inferior feeling.
At such times, were the grossest pieces of onomatopoeic
representation - the song of a bird, the galloping of horses,
the cries of children, or the laughing of demons - to be
introduced into the symphony, I should not be offended. Very
likely I should be pleased; they would afford new points of

224

departure for new trains of romantic feeling or heroic thought. I know very well what has happened. I have been using art as a means to the emotions of life and reading into it the ideas of life. I have been cutting blocks with a razor. I have tumbled from the superb peaks of aesthetic exaltation to the snug foothills of warm humanity. It is a jolly country. No one need be ashamed of enjoying himself there. Only no one who has ever been on the heights can help feeling a little crest-fallen in the cosy valleys. And let no one imagine, because he has made merry in the warm tilth and quaint nooks of romance, that he can even guess at the austere and thrilling raptures of those who have climbed the cold, white peaks of art.

About music most people are as willing to be humble as I am. If they cannot grasp musical form and win from it a pure aesthetic emotion, they confess that they understand music imperfectly or not at all. They recognise quite clearly that there is a difference between the feeling of the musician for pure music and that of the cheerful concert-goer for what music suggests. The latter enjoys his own emotions, as he has every right to do, and recognises

225

their inferiority. Unfortunately, people are apt to be less
modest about their powers of appreciating visual art. Everyone is inclined to believe that out of pictures, at any rate,
he can get all that there is to be got; everyone is ready to
cry 'humbug' and 'impostor' at those who say that more can
be had. The good faith of people who feel pure aesthetic
emotions is called in question by those who have never felt
anything of the sort. It is the prevalence of the representative element, I suppose, that makes the man in the street so
sure that he knows a good picture when he sees one. For
I have noticed that in matters of architecture, pottery,
textiles, etc., ignorance and ineptitude are more willing
to defer to the opinions of those who have been blest with
peculiar sensibility. It is a pity that cultivated and
intelligent men and women cannot be induced to believe
that a great gift of aesthetic appreciation is at least as
rare in visual as in musical art. A comparison of my own
experience in both has enabled me to discriminate very
clearly between pure and impure appreciation. Is it too
much to ask that others should be as honest about their
feelings for pictures as I have been about mine for

226

music? For I am certain that most of those who visit galleries do feel very much what I feel at concerts. They have their moments of pure ecstasy; but the moments are short and unsure. Soon they fall back into the world of human interests and feel emotions, good no doubt, but inferior. I do not dream of saying that what they get from art is bad or nugatory; I say that they do not get the best that art can give. I do not say that they cannot understand art; rather I say that they cannot understand the state of mind of those who understand it best. I do not say that art means nothing or little to them; I say they miss its full significance. I do not suggest for one moment that their appreciation of art is a thing to be ashamed of; the majority of the charming and intelligent people with whom I am acquainted appreciate visual art impurely; and, by theway, the appreciation of almost all great writers has been impure. But provided that there be some fraction of pure aesthetic emotion, even a mixed and minor appreciation of art is, I am sure, one of the most valuable things in the world - so valuable, indeed, that in my giddier moments I have been tempted to

227

believe that art might prove the world's salvation.

Yet, though the echoes and shadows of art enrich the
life of the plains, her spirit dwells on the mountains.
To him who woos, but woos impurely, she returns enriched
what is brought. Like the sun, she warms the good seed
in good soil and causes it to bring forth good fruit.
But only to the perfect lover does she give a new strange
gift - a gift beyond all price. Imperfect lovers bring
to art and take away the ideas and emotions of their own
age and civilisation. In twelfth-century Europe a man
might have been greatly moved by a Romanesque church and
found nothing in a T'ang picture. To a man of a later
age, Greek sculpture meant much and Mexican nothing, for
only to the former could he bring a crowd of associated
ideas to be the objects of familiar emotions. But the
perfect lover, he who can feel the profound significance of
form, is raised above the accidents of time and place. To
him the problems of archaeology, history, and hagiography
are impertinent. If the forms of a work are significant
its provenance is irrelevant. Before the grandeur of those
Sumerian figures in the Louvre he is carried on the same

flood of emotion to the same aesthetic ecstasy as, more than four thousand years ago, the Chaldean lover was carried. It is the mark of great art that its appeal is universal and eternal.[1] Significant form stands charged with the power to provoke aesthetic emotion in anyone capable of feeling it. The ideas of men go buzz and die like gnats; men change their institutions and their customs

---

1 Mr. Roger Fry permits me to make use of an interesting story that will illustrate my view. When Mr. Okakura, the Government editor of The Temple Treasures of Japan, first came to Europe, he found no difficulty in appreciating the pictures of those who from want of will or want of skill did not create illusions but concentrated their energies on the creation of form. He understood immediately the Byzantine masters and the French and Italian Primitives. In the Renaissance painters, on the other hand, with their descriptive pre-occupations, their literary and anecdotic interests, he could see nothing but vulgarity and muddle. The universal and essential quality of art, significant form, was missing, or rather had dwindled to a shallow stream, overlaid and hidden beneath weeds, so the universal response, aesthetic emotion, was not evoked. It was not till he came on to Henri-Matisse that he again found himself in the familiar world of pure art. Similarly, sensitive Europeans who respond immediately to the significant forms of great Oriental art, are left cold by the trivial pieces of anecdote and social criticism so lovingly cherished by Chinese dilettanti. It would be easy to multiply instances did not decency forbid the labouring of so obvious truth.

as they change their coats; the intellectual triumphs of
one age are the follies of another; only great art remains
stable and unobscure. Great art remains stable and unobscure
because the feelings that it awakens are independent of
time and place, because its kingdom is not of this world.
To those who have and hold a sense of the significance of
form what does it matter whether the forms that move them
were created in Paris the day before yesterday or in
Babylon fifty centuries ago? The forms of art are in-
exhaustible; but all lead by the same road of aesthetic
emotion to the same world of aesthetic ecstasy."

AESTHETIC EXPERIENCE AS LACKING ANY COMMON DENOMINATOR

Marshall Cohen's controversial essay threatens the widely-
held thesis that there is a property or set of properties
common to aesthetic experiences. In Cohen's words: "We
do not, I suspect that we cannot, possess a theory about
the essential nature of aesthetic experience, if this
theory is intended (as perhaps it is not) to encompass the
experience of all examples and kinds of art." Using a rich
variety of counter-examples he attempts to undermine the
various traditional criteria of aesthetic experience. Cohen
questions, for example, whether even a characteristic like
unity can be used to distinguish aesthetic from non-aesthetic
experiences. For he observes that the experience of being
badly beaten can have a high degree of unity. Several points
should be noted. First, perhaps to be beaten is not to have
a unified experience. A crime victim is more apt to speak of
his experience as chaotic or muddled, for he is usually unable
to accurately describe the elements of his experience, much
less their interrelationships or the exact order in which they
occurred. Second, even the rare victim, who is able to rec-

231

ollect an integrated character in his experience, may be confusing the disjointed experience that he actually underwent
with a unified account that is the product of an imaginative
reconstruction. Third, even if the experience of being beaten
can be unified, to be unified may be a necessary but not a
sufficient condition for aesthetic experiences. Fourth, Cohen
gives insufficient attention to the transpractical feature
which is preeminent in aesthetic experiences, since it is upon
this that the trans-mundane and transchaotic aspects depend.
For once a person's practical interest is accompanied or superseded by a trans-practical perspective, the experience has an
extraordinary quality (ordinary experiences are marked by a
preoccupation with the practical) and a focus or coherency with
which the usual needs of life normally interfere.

Cohen's article also challenges the thesis that any psychological
state is essential for the would-be aesthete. But it may not be
so difficult to suggest a general state of mind that is necessary
in order to insure that one have an aesthetic experience or the
optimum in such experiences. Defenders of this distinctive state
of mind have traditionally referred to it as an aesthetic attitude.
It is characterized by a positive receptivity to the apprehension of

phenomena either wholly or partly for their presentational value alone. Consider the case of the spectator who brings a sour frame of mind with him to the theatre. Suppose further that the drama being presented is a comedy. Surely, the individual lacks the mental set which is essential to have the appropriate aesthetic experience. Other states of mind, then , can be inimical to the positive, sensitive, receptive outlook which constitutes the aesthetic attitude. So understood, the aesthetic attitude exhibits exactly the degree of generality which Cohen is prone to dismiss as non-existent.

233

AESTHETIC ESSENCE

"It is habitually assumed that there is an element common to
our experiences of works of art (or to experiences called
'aesthetic'). Or if not, it is at least supposed that there
are certain mental states necessary for the having of these
experiences. I call the first assumption the doctrine of
aesthetic experience and the second (in view of its most
frequent form) the doctrine of an aesthetic attitude. A
straightforward commitment to the doctrine of aesthetic
experience may be illustrated by a passage from Roger Fry.
He writes:

> If we compare in our minds responses experienced in
> turn in face of different works of art of the most
> diverse kinds as, for instance, architectural,
> pictorial, musical or literary - we recognize that
> our state of mind in each case has been of a similar
> kind . . . and that (there is something) common
> to all these experiences (and) peculiar to them
> (which) . . . we might conveniently label . . . the
> specifically aesthetic state of mind.[1]

Fry tells us that there is some element common, and peculiar,
to our experience of all works of art. But he does not mention

---

[1]Roger Fry, _Transformations_, Garden City 1956, pp. 1-2.

any marks by which we can identify it. Other writers have
been more specific. Thus, Bullough remarks in his classic
discussion of the various ways, aesthetic and non-aesthetic,
of regarding a fog at sea that so long as we regard it practically (or non-aesthetically) we shall experience anxiety, strain,
and tension. But he holds that once we adopt the aesthetic attitude toward it we shall experience delight and pleasure. This
mode of distinguishing aesthetic from practical experience has
a long history in hedonistic aesthetics (and Bullough's
specific formulation is an obvious attempt to restate in
empirical psychological terms Schopenhauer's conception of
art as a release from the pressures of the Will), but it is
unworkable. Santayana, the acutest of the hedonistic
aestheticians, realized that pleasure characterizes not only
aesthetic but also practical activity. He knew the doctrines
of the Nicomachean Ethics and defined the experience of beauty
as the experience of pleasure objectified, because he knew that
it must be some very special kind of pleasure that could be peculiar to the aesthetic experience of beauty. But, as we may question
whether beauty is, indeed, the essential property of art, we may

236

question whether pleasure, which aestheticians have normally supposed to be characteristic of its apprehension is, truly, an essential feature of aesthetic experience. That beauty is the essence of art has been questioned by Nietzsche and Tolstoy, by Veron and Marinetti, by Eliot and Wittgenstein. And most of them would, I expect, deny that delight or pleasure constitutes the essence of aesthetic experience. Surely, anxiety, tension, and stress, which Bullough takes to be incompatible with aesthetic experience are in fact essential to the effects not only of detective fiction (from Oedipus to the present) but (to suggest only obvious sources) much metaphysical poetry, Sturm und Drang music, and expressionist painting. The muzzles of the battleship Potemkin, pointed at the audience, are positively menancing. The element of truth in theories of psychical distance may be that there are limits to the degrees of intensity that such states as anxiety, tension, and stress may attain and yet remain compatible with aesthetic experience. But if this is true, it is probably equally true of such states as those of pleasure and delight.

It does not seem possible to determine a priori the variety
of sensations, feelings, and attitudes that works of art may en-
gender, and empirical investigation does not seem to have re-
vealed any essential property of those already acknowledged. I
do not wish to deny, on the other hand, that certain sensations,
feelings, and attitudes may be incompatible with the experience
of anything we should conceivably regard as art. But is it worth
nothing that whenever some actual limit has been proposed, in theory or in practice, it has been characteristic of modern artists to
attempt to demonstrate its arbitrariness. If there are not
specific sensations, feelings, or the like that are peculiarly
aesthetic sensations or feelings, it might, nevertheless, be maintained, as by Dewey, that there are certain formal characteristics
of experiences that are peculiarly aesthetic. But this thesis, too,
is difficult to maintain. It is virtually impossible decisively to
refute the various positive suggestions that have been made, for
the terms employed, or the uses made of them, are so vague as to defy
a confident presentation of counter-examples. Nevertheless, one may
wonder whether unity (even unity understood to require that the
experience be pervaded by a single individualizing quality)[2]

---

[2]John Dewey, <u>Art as Experience</u>, New York 1934, pp. 35 ff.

will serve to distinguish aesthetic from non-aesthetic experiences. Surely, the experience of riding a crowded subway or of being badly beaten, has at least as great a degree of unity as (and is more surely pervaded by a single individualizing quality than) the experience of hearing many a sonata or symphonic suite, or of reading many a picaresque novel or chronicle play. And such supplementary characteristics - I choose the least vague - as consummatory quality,[3] or continuity,[4] do not seem any more persuasive. Consummatory quality is more frequently associated with sexual than with aesthetic experience, and various artistic techniques (of which cinematic montage is perhaps the most obvious) are often exploited to create just that gappy, 'breathless', or discontinuous quality that Dewey assigns to practical experience. It is true that a writer such as Dewey would be perfectly content to allow that works of art are not the exclusive sources of aesthetic experience. Yet even those who regard this as a desirable theoretical development may hesitate to subscribe to a formal characterization of aesthetic experience that excludes the

---

[3]Ibid.

[4]Ibid.

experience of central works of art and is satisfied by the experience of brushing one's teeth, or still better, of having them pulled. We do not, and I expect that we cannot, possess a theory about the essential nature of aesthetic experience, if this theory is intended (as perhaps it is not) to encompass the experience of all examples and kinds of art. In what follows I shall, nevertheless, use the phrase 'aesthetic experience' to comprehend the experiences that do character-istically arise from the apprehension of works of art.

There are plainly capacities with which one must be endowed, certain accomplishments one must possess, certain attitudes one must be able to sustain, and certain activities one must be able to perform, if one is to respond adequately to a work of art. Some conditions are logically necessary for particular aesthetic experiences. Thus the man who is tone-deaf cannot enjoy music, and the man who is ignorant of the history o literature cannot apprehend Joyce's Ulysses. It is arguable that other conditions are causally necessary. Perhaps one must be capable of patience to enjoy Proust's novel or an Antonioni film, or of concentration to apprehend a complicated fugue. That such conditions are required for particular aesthetic

experiences no one will deny. But whether, as many aestheticians have suggested, there are certain activities
or psychological states that are always and everywhere
required for (and, even, that insure) having of aesthetic experience may be questioned. It is important,
not only for theoretical reasons, to question such theses.
For, in so far as conditions that are not necessary are
taken to be so, inappropriate training is proposed, and
false instructions are offered, to those who wish to
quicken their aesthetic responses. Quickening one's
aesthetic responses is not a general problem, but a series
of specific problems. In addition, in so far as insufficient
conditions are taken to be sufficient, inadequate training
and preparation are suggested. I am inclined to believe
that there are, in particular, no special activities (such
as contemplating) and no psychological states (such as maintaining 'psychical distance') that are required for having
aesthetic experience. And as these are, perhaps, the most
prestigious candidates I shall discuss them below. But if
it is important to question whether any particular states
are required, it is even more important to question whether

241

we can know, in advance of the fact, what activities or
states of mind will insure the proper apprehension of
a work of art. And beyond activities and states of mind,
what sensory capacities, what knowledge, courage, or
imagination.

The choice of contemplation as the essential precondition (or, indeed, the essential element) of aesthetic experience is, doubtless, influenced by the
traditional opposition of the vita activa to the vita
contemplativa. In the modern version that concerns us,
however, it is neither philosophical nor religious contemplation that is contrasted with the life of action, but
aesthetic contemplation that is contrasted with physical
activity, intellectual labour, and practical interest.
(In a transitional figure, such as Schopenhauer, the
distinction between philosophical or religious and aesthetic contemplation tends to fail.) This elaborate history
has left us with a profoundly confused and (as Maritain
suggests) perverted term. And this makes a discussion of
aesthetic theories in which the concept of contemplation
figures crucially exceptionally difficult. The term 'contem-

plation' is used in aesthetic contexts by many writers simply to comprehend whatever conditions they suppose necessary for obtaining aesthetic experience. But when the term is employed in this manner the question is effectively begged whether there is any feature common to the bewildering variety of psychological states, and even physical activities, that may be required for obtaining the varieties of aesthetic experience. So, too, is the question begged whether the term 'contemplation' can serve both this broad purpose and yet be understood to preclude (as it is normally understood by these same writers to preclude) various physical actions, intellectual operations, or moral interests. There is no point from which one can contemplate Wright's Guggenheim Museum or Le Corbusier's Carpenter Center (the aesthetic experience requires physical movement), no way of appropriating a novel of Broch's or Mann's without engaging in the meditation and cogitation that Richard of St Victor contrasts with contemplation, no way of feeling the excitement of Goya's "The Disasters of War" or Dostoyevsky's The Possessed without exercising those moral and political interests that are typically contrasted with aesthetic, ironic, or disinterested contemplation.

It would not do, however, to represent all theorists as presenting us with so unsatisfactory a situation. No contemporary aesthetician has, so far as I know, investigated the subject of contemplation with the kind of detail that can be found in Richard of St Victor, who in addition to distinguishing contemplation from meditation and cogitation noticed its six varieties. But the term 'contemplation' is at least employed with some sense of its non-technical use by an occasional writer on the visual arts. Thus, Pudovkin, who is interested in establishing that 'the camera compels the spectator to see as the director wishes' knows that the camera 'is charged with a conditional relation to the object shot. Now, urged by heightened interest, it delves into details; now it contemplates the general whole of the picture'.[5] Pudovkin observes the difference between delving into and contemplating a scene. And if the camera can force us to see in these different ways so, I think, can the painter. If one ought to contemplate a Redon or a Rothko, one ought to scrutinize the Westminster Psalter, survey a Tiepolo ceiling, regard a Watteau,

---

[5]V.I. Pudovkin, Film Technique and Film Acting, London 1958, pp. 154-155.

and peer at a scene of Breughel.[6] If we attend to these distinctions we shall be in a position to deny that we must contemplate these works to have a proper aesthetic experience of them. Nor is it the case, as might be suspected, that writers who observe these distinctions do so because they are innocent of philosophical plans for the concept of contemplation. Here we come upon an instance where a form of doctrine of aesthetic essence is not independent of a theory about the nature of art.

From the Greeks onward it has been supposed that contemplation requires special kinds of objects, and sometimes that only contemplation is capable of discerning these objects. Modern aesthetics reflects this tradition. For the artistically embodied Ideas of Schopenhauer and the Significant Forms of Bell and Fry require contemplation. And it is assumed that in so far as other modes of vision are present they must be directed to non-aesthetic or aesthetically irrelevant aspects of the work of art. A hint of this may be found in Roger Fry's

---

[6]Cf. Paul Ziff, 'Reason in Art Criticism', reprinted in Joseph Margolis, ed., Philosophy Looks at the Arts, New York 1962, pp. 164ff. I am grateful to Professor Ziff, as well as to Professors Rogers Albritton and Stanley Cavell, for reading and criticizing an earlier version of this manuscript.

discussion of Breughel's 'Carrying of the Cross'. 'We are
invited,' he writes, 'by the whole method of treatment, to
come close and peer at each figure in turn and read from it
those details which express its particular state of mind
so that we may gradually, almost as we might in a novel,
bring them together to build up a highly complex psychological
structure.'[7] Fry dislikes Breughel's kind of painting, and
what he dislikes about it is what makes it proper to 'peer at
it' and 'read it closely' (rather than 'contemplate' it as
one would a Cezanne). For peering displays a psychological
rather than an aesthetic, interest, and Breughel is literary
even novelistic, rather than painterly and significantly
formalistic. In a word, his painting is non-aesthetic in its
appeal, and this is reflected in the fact that it is apprehended
by the allegedly non-aesthetic activity of peering. We must
however, stand with Pudovkin and Breughel for the right to delve
and peer. The notion that contemplation is the essential condition
of aesthetic experience is often no more than a reflection of the
theorist's negligent assumption that the rapt Oriental contemplatin

---

[7]Fry, op. cit., p. 19.

246

a Chinese vase is the paradigm of aesthetic experience. When it is not, it is likely to enshrine partisan tastes such as Fry's.

In addition to implying misleading accounts of the conditions of aesthetic experience, psychological versions of the theory of aesthetic essence have provided one of the main motivations for false conceptions of the nature and elements of art itself. The notion that some psychological state, such as Bullough's psychical distance is the necessary (and, indeed, the sufficient) condition of aesthetic experience has led both Bullough and Mrs. Langer to attempt to explain its presence or absence by some doctrine about the nature of elements of art. Mrs. Langer, for instance constructs her doctrine that the work of art is an appearance or illusion in order to explain how art imposes an aesthetic 'attitude' and how, by its very nature, it cannot sustain a practical interest.[8] (She falsely assimilates work of art

---

[8]Susanne Langer, Feeling and Form, New York 1953. See the discussion of Mrs. Langer's views in Marshall Cohen, "Appearance and the Aesthetic Attitude', The Journal of Philosophy, vol. 56 (November 5, 1959), pp. 921-924. The article is reprinted in Marvin Levich, ed., Aesthetics and the Philosophy of Criticism, New York 1963.

to shadows and rainbows, and forgets the practical uses of signs and wonders.) Bullough's doctrine is less extreme, and despite some remarks in the tradition of Schiller, he does not clearly commit himself to the view of art as appearance or illusion. Nevertheless, it is his view that various features of works of art either encourage, or discourage, the occurence of a state of mind that he calls psychical distance. I wish to argue that there is no need to assume the presence of such a state as a precondition or element of aesthetic experience. In addition, I shall argue that the interpretation of works of art on the assumption that the function of certain of their stylistic traits is to induce this state leads to a misinterpretation of them.

The psychological state supposed to be the necessary condition of aesthetic experience has been described by Prall as involving a loss of the sense of one's body, by Schopenhauer as involving a loss of the sense of one's self and by Ethel Puffer as being akin to hypnosis. (Schopenhauer discourages an appeal to spiritous drinks or opium to achieve

248

this state, and suggests, rather, a cold bath and a night's sleep.) Bullough's suggestion, if less patently false, is yet communicated in a metaphor susceptible of many interpretations. The most typical interpretation is one under which we may say that James or Brecht, or their readers, maintain their distance from Verena Tarrant or from Galy Gay. However, in this sense, we also say that distance is not maintained from Isabel Archer or Mother Courage. But this cannot be the proper interpretation of Bullough's term, for a lack of distance in this sense is fully compatible with aesthetic experience. (And we may contradict those critics who suppose that the maintenance of distance makes The Bostonians a greater novel than The Portrait of a Lady. I do not know whether anyone has made so bold a move in the case of Brecht.) How, then, are we to interpret Bullough? While he thinks of distance as a psychic state, we know that on occasion he relates it in an exceptionally straightforward way to certain behavioural manifestations. When we suffer tension, stress, or anxiety we tend to react practically to the situation. It is his view that certain elements of works of art arouse such feelings; in particular, those

representing humanly compelling situations. For this
reason works of art also include other elements to attenuate or 'distance' those feelings and to inhibit action.
In the case of the theatre, for instance, these elements
would include the raised stage and the use of costumes and
verse. Now Bullough mentions as a clear case of the loss
of distance the yokel who leaps upon the stage to save
the hapless heroine.[9] Bullough would have us believe
that the pressure of his feelings induces the yokel to gain
the stage and that the operation of the distancing factors
has kept the rest of the audience in their seats. But
can we not imagine that the yokel has acted cooly out of an
ignorant sense of honour while the carriage-trade has
remained in its place seething with emotion? (I assume for
the purpose of this discussion that their seething is compatible with the maintenance of sufficient psychical distance.)
The operative factors here may not be feelings at all, but
rather the presence and absence of knowledge of what a play is

---

[9] See the discussion of Bullough's views in George Dickie, 'Is
Psychology Relevant to Aesthetics?' The Philosophical Review, vol.
71 (July 1962), pp. 297-300.

and of how one behaves in the theatre. If so, the satisfaction of at least this behavioural criterion of 'psychical' distance, namely, staying put, may be compatible with a wide range of feelings or with none at all. And, indeed, this assumption comports best with the introspective situation.

If knowledge of what a play is should be sufficient to keep the yokel seated, and if no particular feelings or emotions are required to keep the audience in its seats, it will be inappropriate to account for certain elements of a work of art by their tendency to enforce, and others by their tendency to undermine, such psychical states. If the yokel learns what it is to go to a play we shall be able to do the play in a field, without costumes, and in prose, and still expect him to react properly. Thus, the function of the raised stage, costumes, and verse need not be to keep him seated. Indeed, the very stylistic qualities that Bullough supposes to be distancing because of their anti-realistic nature may operate in precisely the opposite fashion. Let us take the theatrical case. The raised stage, appropriate for the performance of Ibsen's plays, tends to make the playgoer less conscious of the rest of the audience. And allowing him to peep into a

251

realistic set peopled with literally costumed characters actually adds to the 'realism' of the play. (Hence the habitual failure of arena-stage productions of Ibsen.) Nor can it plausibly be maintained that the general function of verse is to attenuate responses to the represented events. This does not seem to have been the effect of Aeschylus' verse on the women who gave birth at his plays, or of Shakespeare's on Dr. Johnson's reaction to the final scene of King Lear. Alternatively, O'Neill's prosy climaxes (Lavinia's 'O fiddlesticks!') hardly seem to increase the reality of these scenes.

If Bullough's suggestions are often misleading, they are even more often irrelevant. He supposes-it is only an extension of his treatment of the yokel-that anti-realistic (highly-distanced) styles are required mainly to inhibit and to render aesthetic the practical impulses of relatively primitive and unsophisticated peoples. But his hypothesis is quite irrelevant to the problem of the modern anti-realistic style that has occasioned the brilliant speculations of Ortega and Malraux. For this 'dehumanized' style is the expression, as Ortega indicates, not of the aesthetically unsophisticated

masses, but, on the contrary, of an aesthetic elite.[10] And
Malraux's argument is of a logical type that Bullough's mode
of analysis does not even allow him. For where Bullough's
method would lead him to find in the modern renewal of the
anti-humanistic or 'transcendental' style a (psychological)
purpose similar to that served by this style in the past,
it is open to Malraux to suggest that this style has a (non-
psychological) purpose exactly opposite to that which is previously served. (It is, he thinks, a 'photographic negative'
of previous transcendental styles and serves to express a new
humanism rather than to cancel a discredited one.)[11] The possibility of offering quite different accounts of the functions
of similar stylistic elements on different occasions and of
finding these explanations not in psychological factors but,
perhaps, in considerations of history or of Weltanschauung
seems all to the good. Bullough's attempt to relate such explanations to the fortunes of some otiose and unidentifiable

---

[10]Jose Ortega y Gasset, The Dehumanization of Art, Garden
City 1956.

[11] Andre Malraux, The Voices of Silence, Garden City 1953;
Joseph Frank 'Malraux's Metaphysics', The Sewanee Review, vol.
70 (Autumn 1962), p. 646.

psychological state cannot be regarded as useful procedures. Like Mrs. Langer's theory that all works of art are appearances or illusions, Bullough's notion that stylistic elements should be understood as increasing or decreasing distance may be dismissed with its questionable motivation. There is no way of determining the precondition of all aesthetic experience just as there is no way of knowing what qualities such experience must bear."

SELECTED BIBLIOGRAPHY

Aldrich, Virgil, _Philosophy of Art_, Chap. 1, Englewood Cliffs, N.J.: Prentice Hall, 1963.

Beardsley, Monroe C., _Aesthetics: Problems in the Philosophy of Criticism_, pp. 552-554. New York: Harcourt, Brace & World, Inc., 1958.

Bell, Clive, _Art_, New York: G. P. Putnam's Sons, 1958.

Dickie, George, _Aesthetics: An Introduction_, Chaps. 5, 6. Indianapolis and New York: The Bobbs-Merrill Company, Inc., 1971.

_____. _Art and the Aesthetic: An Institutional Analysis_, Chaps. 2-6, 8. Ithica and London: Cornell University Press 1974.

Ducasse, Curt John, _The Philosophy of Art_, New York: Dover Publications, Inc., 1966.

Lipman, Matthew, ed., _Contemporary Aesthetics_, Part Three. Boston: Allyn and Bacon, Inc., 1973.

Munro, Thomas, _Oriental Aesthetics_, Cleveland, Ohio: The Press of Western Reserve University, 1965.

Osborne, Harold, _The Art of Appreciation_, Chap. 2. London: Oxford University Press, 1970.

Prall, D. W., _Aesthetic Judgment_, New York: Thomas Y. Crowell Co., 1929.

Rader, Melvin and Betram Jessup, _Art and Human Values_, Chap. 3. Englewood Cliffs, N. J.: Prentice Hall, 1976.

Stolnitz, Jerome, _Aesthetics and Philosophy of Art Criticism_, Part I. Boston, Houghton Mifflin, 1960.

Suzuki, D. T., _Zen and Japanese Culture_, New York: Princeton
    University Press, 1959.

Tillman, Frank A. and Steven M. Cahn, eds., _Philosophy of Art
    and Aesthetics: From Plato to Wittgenstein_, pp. 762-763.
    New York, Evanston, and London: Harper and Row, 1969.

Tolstoy, Leo, _What Is Art_? Trans. Aylmer Maude. Indianapolis
    and New York: The Bobbs-Merrill Company, Inc., 1960.

Vivas, Eliseo and Murray Krieger, eds., _The Problems of
    Aesthetics_, pp. 277-411. New York: Holt, Rinehart and
    Winston, 1953.